Electric Guitar Setups

CW01033131

by Hideo Kamimoto
author of *Complete Guitar Repair*

A richly detailed and illustrated guide to getting the best sound and feel
from your electric or acoustic-electric guitar.

Amsco Publications
New York/London/Sydney

ACKNOWLEDGEMENTS

In the early days of researching the guitars to be included as examples in this project, it quickly became apparent that many of the more interesting and important (older) ones were simply not as common as they used to be. While the majority of the makes and models described in the following pages have come into my shop over the years, somehow the importance of documenting and photographing the instruments (at the time) just doesn't seem very urgent when you're repairing guitars for a living. In any event, working on guitars in the old days—the early sixties for me—gave me enough challenges just in trying to figure out how to repair them (for there were no repair books of any kind), let alone leaving me time to consider their historic and collectible value.

The problem of assembling, for this book, a large collection of guitars for examination and photos was solved through the generous assistance of the following individuals and stores: Dan Aroni and Gary Wineroth (Guitar Showcase, San Jose, California); Phillip Kirby; Bob Kothenbeutel; Vallis Kolbeck (Al's Guitarville, Seattle); Bill Stapleton, Kevin Fallon, and Ben Bryan (American Music, Seattle).

Bill Stapleton, Phillip Kirby, Paul Lupus, and Dave McCumiskey provided assistance with proofreading, comments, and suggestions. I would also like to thank American Precision Metal Works (Kahler tremolo) and Floyd Rose and Fender Musical Instruments (Floyd Rose tremolo) for assistance regarding their tremolo systems.

A special thanks to Bill Stapleton, who contributed to the chapter on tremolo systems (Chapter 7). Bill's familiarity with the historic and musical importance of many popular (and not-so-popular) makers and models also helped greatly in defining the examples included in these pages.

All photographs are by Hideo Kamimoto, except for those of the Peterson strobe tuners, which were supplied by the Peterson Electro-Musical Products Corporation.

Cover photography by Retna Ltd.
Interior design and layout by Len Vogler

Order No. AM 91473
US International Standard Book Number: 0.8256.1379.5
UK International Standard Book Number: 0.7119.3710.9

Exclusive Distributors:
Music Sales Corporation
257 Park Avenue South, New York, NY 10010 USA
Music Sales Limited
8/9 Frith Street, London W1V 5TZ England
Music Sales Pty. Limited
120 Rothschild Street, Rosebery, Sydney, NSW 2018, Australia

Printed in the United States of America by
Vicks Lithograph and Printing Corporation

CONTENTS

PREFACE

While guitar setup work is not difficult to understand or perform, it does often call for detailed information and instruction. Much of this has not been readily available or is not specific enough to be useful to a player interested in setting up his or her own instrument.

This book hopes to fill that gap. I hope that it will be helpful to anyone with an interest in this type of work. If you are a guitarist, doing your own setup will lead to a better understanding of the strengths and limitations of your instrument, and thereby give you more confidence in your playing. If you are a repairperson, a grounding in the fundamentals of setup and action work can serve as a platform for other guitar repair skills. Throughout the book I have included appropriate theory and reasoning to back up every procedure so that you will be able to apply any particular skill learned here to a variety of situations.

I would suggest skimming through the book to get an overview of the subjects covered before settling down to those specific chapters that interest you. Some of the tips given here are a standard part of guitar repair knowledge. Others are based on my own professional experience. My goal is to help you to find practical solutions to setup and action problems on real guitars—and have a little fun learning about your instrument in the process.

DEDICATION

to Sharon

INTRODUCTION

A well-set up electric guitar plays in tune and with good intonation, responds smoothly and easily to your playing style, and sends out the amplified sound that you want. Defining the goal is easy enough: everyone wants a guitar that plays easily and sounds great. The means to that end is a little trickier. You need to know not only the "nuts and bolts" of how to work on a guitar but also the principles that underpin each particular operation. And you need to be able to judge what kinds of work you can do yourself and what might best be left to the professional repairperson.

All guitars need to be set up, from the basic one they receive at the factory to the periodic work required to maintain them in good playing condition as they experience normal wear and climatic conditions. Of course, one of the most important reasons for adjusting (and readjusting) a setup is to adapt an instrument to your playing style.

You will find in this book not just a basic "how-to" guide, but also plenty of detailed discussion of the reasoning behind each step of the setup process. In this way you will be able to adjust to the idiosyncrasies of any guitar that you may work on. As you will discover, no two guitars will behave exactly alike. Two guitars of the same make and model will require slightly different adjustments for the same action, even when strung with the same make and gauge of strings.

Electric guitars, while sharing many of the same setup and action requirements as acoustic guitars, pose additional difficulties because of the pickup and electronic circuitry involved. Setting up the electronics should be integrated into the larger process. An electric guitar setup introduces some interesting variables because adjustment of the pickups affects both action and intonation in addition to the obvious changes in amplified tone and volume. As you will learn, working with the pickups (as a part of the overall setup process) involves knowing how as well as when to adjust. I will spend some time discussing conventional pickups as well as providing details on installation and adjustment of several popular transducers for electric-acoustic conversions.

In keeping with the aim of the book to provide you with specific information and adjustment tips on popular guitars that you will be likely to work on or own, we will take a look at a selection of the most popular guitar makes, such as the famous Fender and Gibson designs. A large body of knowledge has been built up around these instruments. The principles involved in working on them can be applied again when working on similar designs.

But not all setup work involves the classics. Many advances in guitar design have been made in recent years. In particular, the locking tremolo bridges popularized by Floyd Rose and Gary Kahler demand attention. Locking nuts and string locks are often installed together with a locking tremolo bridge as a system.

If you are in the market for another guitar either used or new (and who isn't?), the information in this book can help you check out your prospective purchase for defects or problem areas. Since guitars can sometimes require costly repairs, knowing the potential for problems beforehand will put you in a better position to get the best instrument for your money—or, what may be just as valuable, tell you when to pass up that "bargain" and keep on looking. Some things which may superficially seem trivial, such as a "slightly" warped neck, can become a major pain (in the neck?) if you can't tell simple adjustment problems apart from major repair and restoration.

Basic setup work is the bread and butter of most repair shops just as are tune-ups for an auto mechanic's. While some complex setups are probably best left to the professional repairperson, particularly those that involve repairs rather than adjustments, there is no reason why you can't do the basic stuff yourself. With the proper tools, study, and time, you'll end up with a guitar that will play the way *you* want it to, and you will have fun working on and learning about your instrument.

But why do a setup at all when all of this is taken care of at the factory? Well, it is true that all factories do a basic setup on their instruments so that they will be reasonably playable for most players. Yet, you can easily understand that because of the time-consuming nature of setting up a guitar to standards beyond that of the most basic nature, most factories choose to spend less time on setups than might be considered ideal. In fairness to the factory, their setup work can't take into account the wide range of playing styles, string gauges, and actions that their instruments will be subjected to. The factories are working for a nonexistent average player.

This so-called average action (read as "fairly high") covers up small inconsistencies in fret height which would show up as fret buzzes if set up to tighter tolerances. Though we all would like new guitars to play perfectly straight out of the box, a more realistic approach would be to consider a factory instrument in reasonable playing condition as only a starting point. We can take up where the factory left off and do the extra work, both basic and detail, which will customize the instrument to our specific needs.

On the other hand, used instruments may or may not be in reasonable condition when you begin your setup adjustments. Whereas new factory instruments that fail the "reasonable playing condition" test can be returned or exchanged, used instruments must first be examined to determine whether or not any repairs must be done as a part of setting up. You will have to use some judgement here, based on the information in this book or upon the advice of a repairperson.

While some guitar factories, especially the ones that produce high-end instruments, can do an excellent setup job, you can always assume that an instrument can be improved to suit your own preferences. Sometimes these improvements can be startling. In these pages, we are going to take a new guitar in "factory adjusted" condition, or, in the case of a used guitar, the condition it was in when you bought it, and try to get it to play as close to perfection as possible.

1
THE THREE PARTS OF THE BASIC SETUP

A basic setup procedure consists of three parts: action adjustments, electronic adjustments (where applicable), and intonation adjustments. These elements are interrelated. Each will affect one or both of the others, so that if they are not done in the correct order later adjustments will affect the earlier ones and vice versa.

You can avoid problems if you are careful to do your setup in such a way that each step does not affect the previous one. Stick to the order described below and save yourself a lot of frustration and wasted time.

ACTION

Strings

Restring your guitar with strings that you will be using "permanently" and tune to pitch. The type of string and tuning you use will influence every aspect of your setup. Even if your present strings are only a few days old a restringing is still a good idea. This is especially important when using light rock-and-roll gauges. Depending on playing conditions (heat, humidity, sweaty fingers), strings can go bad in just a few hours.

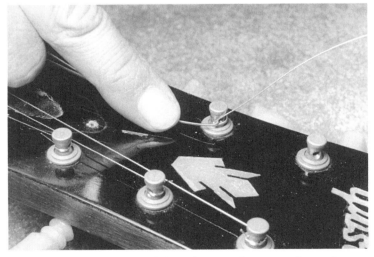

Restringing the guitar: "Lock" the string onto the post as shown. Leave enough slack so that two or three turns can be evenly wound down toward the ferrule, as on the first, second, and third strings.

Trussrod

Begin your action adjustment with the trussrod if your guitar has one. The trussrod adjustment will counteract the upward pull of the string (and bowing of the neck), and will allow you to incorporate a small amount of clearance in the middle of the fingerboard so that a vibrating string can move naturally without hitting the frets. The term used to describe this clearance is neck or fingerboard *relief* (for a detailed discussion of the theory and practical application of neck relief, refer to Appendix A).

Checking the action: Sight down the neck to check basic neck angle and straightness.

The upward pull on the neck by the strings and the downward pull by the trussrod affects the action at the nut and at the bridge, but don't make the mistake of using trussrod adjustments to try to change string height. The trussrod is there to counteract the string tension and to set the neck relief. If you use it to alter string height you will more than likely end up with a lot of buzzes all over the fingerboard.

In most cases, making adjustments is simple. Use the correct type of wrench, and find the trussrod. The adjustment nut can be found at the peghead (sometimes behind a cover) or at the base of the neck (through the soundhole in the case of most acoustic-electric guitars). Many solidbody electrics have a recess in the body at the base of the neck to permit access to the trussrod nut.

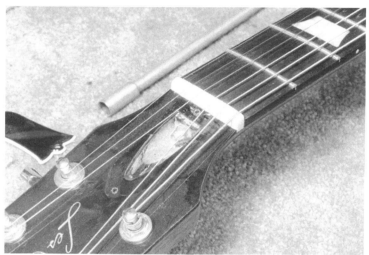

Adjusting the trussrod: Adjust the trussrod first. The string notches in the nut should be adjusted after all trussrod adjustments have been completed.

Many Fender guitars and Fender copies, however, have nuts partially covered by the body and pickguard. The only way to properly adjust these necks is to loosen the strings, unbolt the neck and push it up far enough to expose the nut. This process might have to be repeated several times before the rod is correctly set, since you have to tune up the strings to check up on each adjustment. But you can console yourself with the knowledge that the trussrod probably won't have to be touched again for a long time (and this goes for all guitars) unless you change the string gauge.

Go slowly, adjusting in increments of an eighth of a turn or so (clockwise to tighten for less relief and counterclockwise to loosen for more relief) at a time. With each adjustment, check your progress with a straightedge held between the first and twelfth frets. Your goal is to get the relief within acceptable limits without reaching the rod's breaking point or making it so loose that it rattles. If the rod is working correctly, this shouldn't be a problem. If you really have to twist the nut and still not much is happening, there are most likely serious problems with the neck or trussrod or both and it would be best to have the guitar checked out by a good repairperson.

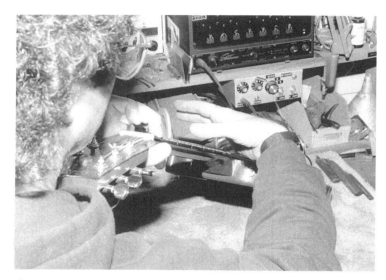

Checking neck relief: You can do a "rough" check on neck relief by holding a string down at the first and thirteenth frets and "tapping" the string down at the sixth fret. The string movement (and clicking sound of the string hitting the frets) will indicate the amount of relief.

If your guitar's trussrod has been properly set in the past, most new adjustments can be done with less than a quarter turn in either direction from the present position. On rock-and-roll guitars with very light strings, you'll probably need no more than an eighth of a turn. So go easy and be sure to retune the guitar as you go along. Maintaining tuning (read: string tension) is crucial to accurate trussrod adjustment. For basic adjustments, follow the recommendations given in the chart below. (If you are interested in relief calculations for all actions and all frets, see the *Relief Calculations* chart in Appendix A.)

Basic Neck Relief Settings

Type of Guitar (playing style)	Action (chart 2)	Relief (inch)
Rock & Roll	Med-Low	0.010
Standard and Jazz	Med-Low	0.013
Acoustic-Electric	Med-Low	0.013
Classical-Electric	Med-Low	0.023
Electric Bass	Med-Low	0.020

If your guitar does not have an adjustable rod there is not much you can do about adjusting neck relief or neck warp beyond changing to different gauges of strings. You may have to have a heatbend done to the neck (in the repair shop), or you might be able to get by with a fretmill. Generally though, most guitars with non-adjustable necks are acoustics or acoustic-electrics that usually are not as sensitive to precise amounts of neck relief as rock-and-roll instruments. Due to their heavier strings and higher actions, acoustics can be made to play well so long as the neck is reasonably close to normal (no back bow and reasonable relief). Some additional "fine tuning," however, can be done with a fretmill if your frets are in good shape.

Finally, keep in mind the following thoughts on trussrod adjustments. Always hold the guitar in playing position when checking for straightness. The neck can flex a great deal from just the weight of the neck and body when not supported properly. This is especially true for electric basses. By holding the instrument in playing position you produce the same stress on the guitar as when it is actually played, and your trussrod and action adjustments will be more accurate.

Measuring neck relief: Check neck relief after changing strings or adjusting the trussrod.

It's a good idea to periodically check the neck relief as you do the remaining setup work. It can change, especially after alterations in trussrod tension or substantial changes in string height at the bridge. It is very common to have to touch up the trussrod adjustment several times during the course of a setup.

Nut

Work on the nut consists of adjusting the slots that control string height so that each string will be neither too high nor too low to the first fret. This adjustment must follow all major trussrod adjustments because the flexing of the neck as the rod is adjusted will change the distance between the string and the first fret. For this reason, you must also have all the strings tuned up to pitch before starting the adjustment procedure. For this work you will need:

- A small needle file;

- A small extra-slim taper file, 7 inch;

- A small thin dovetail-type saw, such as a German model-maker's saw, or an X-acto saw—these should only be used for cutting the notches for plain steel strings;

- A mill smooth file, 8 inch;

- Sandpaper, from 220 grit to 600 grit.

You can get sets of files designed specifically for guitars from various luthiers' supply houses. These work very well but are expensive. The small needle file will be used to cut the notches for wound steel strings as well as nylon strings. It too can be found at luthiers' supply houses, but also at jewelers' supply houses, craft and hobby shops, and larger hardware stores. The extra-slim taper file, the mill smooth file, and the sandpaper are all easily obtainable at hardware stores. The German model-maker's saw (Blitz is a common brand) can be found at luthiers' supply houses and some hardware stores. The X-acto saw can be purchased at most hobby shops. Blades are available in several thicknesses, matching the diameters of the most commonly used plain steel strings.

Actual filing technique is straightforward. After tuning all the strings to pitch, check the height of the string notches by pressing each string down between the second and third frets. Observe the clearance between the string and the first fret. Raise any string that touches the fret. For the average guitar the clearance on the first (high E) string should be in the range of six thousandths of an inch. For an electric bass, this clearance should be around a hundredth of an inch. Clearance should gradually increase two or three thousandths more as you go toward the lower strings. For additional details refer to the *Relief Calculations* chart in Appendix A (under "first fret interval").

Measuring string height at the nut: The string height at the nut is checked by pressing the string (the fifth string is being checked in the photo) down between the second and third frets. There should be a small amount of clearance over the first fret.

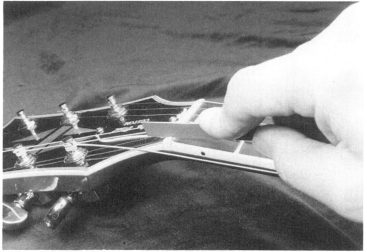

Filing the string notches: Angle the file downward toward the peghead. Too shallow an angle will lead to string buzz and loss of sustain.

You don't have to measure the precise clearance for each string; it is sufficient to observe that you have a "little" clearance between the string and the fret. A trick many repairpeople use is to lightly tap the string down on the first fret while fretting the string between the second and third frets. You will hear a distinctive "tink" if the string is close to but not touching the first fret. It does no harm to have a little clearance to spare so that when you play harder on the open strings you will not get extra fret buzz. On the other hand, don't leave the strings too high, or you will get intonation problems as well as a hard action.

Electric basses will need a little extra clearance (add two or three thousandths) over that required for guitars. Some acoustic guitars may also require a little more. In both cases this is because of the extra relief and action height that these instruments require.

If your strings are too high, file the notch using a file of the correct diameter or the one that comes closest. Lift the string out of the notch with your fingers. Put one hand in front of the nut and one hand behind, lift the string straight up, and lay it down adjacent to the notch. File the notch from the fingerboard gently downward toward the peghead. For best tone and sustain, you will want to make the maximum string pressure be on the front edge of the nut, where it touches the fingerboard. On the back side of the nut the slot should gently fall away so that the string will slide smoothly.

If you have a lot of material to remove, start with the extra-slim taper file, switching to the needle files, saws, and nut files as you get closer to the final adjustment. If the string is slightly wider than your file, you can file with a little side pressure to widen the slot. Adjust your filing motion so that the slot diameter remains smooth and round. You can also widen the slots for the plain strings with the saws, though with these slots the range of adjustment is much more limited. Check your adjustments often as you get to the final height. It is a lot of work to raise a string notch that has been filed too low, so proceed carefully, making sure that the string is not hanging up in the notch and checking that the trussrod setting and tuning has not changed. It is vitally important that you maintain a slight downward angle in the string notch as it goes toward the peghead. A notch filed at too shallow an angle will allow the string to move around in the nut as it vibrates, resulting in a marked loss of tone and sustain. A notch that is too wide will also cost you the same loss of tone and sustain. Because the nut slots wear out over a period of time, you can often restore a guitar's open-string tone simply by touching up the nut slots at the correct angle and diameter.

If a string slot happens to be too low, either through wear or because of careless filing, it is possible to save the nut without having to replace it. Sand the nut and collect some of the dust. Put a drop of cyanoacrylate glue in the slot and add the dust. Put another drop on top of the dust and harden it with an accelerator. Clean up the area and file the slot to the right depth. Keep in mind that this type of repair is good only for very minor height adjustments, since the filled area will not be as hard as the original and will tend to wear more quickly. If several slots are too low, it would be best to remove the entire nut and either shim it up or replace it.

When the process of notching the nut results in deep string grooves, remove the excess material by filing and sandpapering. Although the string only needs to be seated in the notch by about half its diameter, in actual practice it is better to have the strings a little deeper in order to prevent them from popping out when you bend strings and pull off. About two-thirds of the string diameter in the slot should be about right for the wound strings, and flush with the top of the nut for the plain strings.

The finished nut: With notches cut to the proper height and excess material removed over the strings, your nut should look like this. If you have a guitar with a shallow peghead angle (as on many bolt-on style necks), you should leave more material above the strings in order to help prevent the strings from popping out.

Bridge

The final step in setting up an action is to adjust the string height at the bridge. Because string gauge and tuning as well as trussrod and nut adjustments all influence string height, it's important to save the bridge adjustment for last.

Shaping the nut: Remove excess material from the nut. Besides the improved appearance, the strings will slide more easily in the notches.

Take a moment to think about your requirements and how high or low you want your action to be. Your playing style, choice of music, and individual preference in action is likely to be different from that of another person who may be using the same guitar and gauge of strings. If you don't already have a specific preference for action height, the *Guitar and Electric Bass Actions* chart can give you some ideas regarding typical actions. Use these figures as starting points and modify them to suit your playing style. A lot depends upon how hard you play your instrument, as well as on your tolerance for fret buzz.

Guitar and Electric Bass Actions chart

Action		<R&R (Electric) Std>			Acoustic (Steel String)			Classical (nylon string)			Electric Bass		
64ths	Range	L	M	H	L	M	H	L	M	H	L	M	H
1	1-2												
2	2-3	●											
3	3-4	●											
4	4-6		●		●						●		
5	5-7		●		●						●		
6	6-8			●		●		●				●	
7	7-9			●		●		●				●	
8	8-10						●		●				●
9	9-11						●		●				●
10	10-12									●			
11	11-14									●			
12	12-14												

This chart may be used as a reference point when setting up actions. All action measurements are in sixty-fourths of an inch and are measured at the twelfth fret (from the bottom of the string to the top of the fret). Under the column "Range," the low figure is for the highest (treble) string and the high figure is for the lowest (bass) string. If you aren't sure about which action to use, try starting with the lower end of the medium range and afterwards adjust to suit your own preference. While the range of actions given in this chart will suit most players, those who have specialized requirements in strings and playing styles may require differing adjustments.

It's common practice to indicate string heights in increments of sixty-fourths of an inch over the fingerboard at the twelfth fret. For example, an action of 4 and 6 means four sixty-fourths of an inch between the bottom of the first string and the top of the twelfth fret and six sixty-fourths of an inch between the bottom of the sixth (low E) string and top of the twelfth fret.

Keep in mind that while a sixty-fourth of an inch is a small distance, a change of this magnitude can equal a quarter to a third or more of the whole string height when string actions are only three or four sixty-fourths to start with. Half a sixty-fourth, or phrases like "just a shade over" or "a bit less than" have real meaning when dealing with actions. Measuring in thousandths of an inch is more precise but is not the *lingua franca* of measuring fretted instrument actions.

The general rule for adjusting actions is that, going from the first to the sixth strings, there should be a gradual increase in height. This should follow the radius (curve) of the fingerboard (where applicable). There should also be gradually increasing string heights toward the bass strings. On guitar bridges that have individually adjustable saddles, simply adjust the overall height and string-to-string heights with the individual saddles. Another bridge style, typified by the Floyd Rose tremolo bridges, has the saddles held down by screws. These screws hold the saddles in place after they have been adjusted for intonation. It is possible to adjust the saddles individually by using thin shims

(metal usually), though for most guitars the built-in radius compensation and the basic bridge height adjustment screws allow for adequate adjustment.

Measuring the action: Check the action at the twelfth fret. Be sure to check every string; the action should rise gradually and be highest at the sixth string.

Though the popular Gibson Tune-O-Matic bridges adjust for overall height by thumbwheels at either end of the bridge, the saddles themselves can be adjusted over a limited range by notching them with the same files and saws used for notching nuts. This is an important adjustment because the saddles are rarely notched to conform correctly to the curvature of the fingerboard. As a general rule for all bridges, adjust individual saddle height whenever possible. Always measure the clearance between the string and the twelfth fret. Estimating by eye is rarely accurate enough to obtain the gradual string-to-string height changes necessary for the best actions.

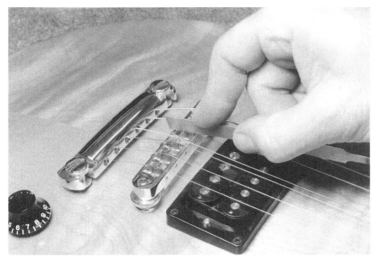

Adjusting the saddles: Adjust the string saddles and bridge base (where applicable) so that the difference in action from string to string is smooth and gradual.

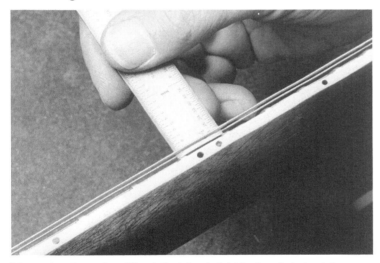

Measuring the action: The sixth-string height in the photo is at 5, or five sixty-fourths of an inch above the top of the fret.

Acoustic-electric guitars and all guitars that have a single fixed saddle for all six strings require that the saddle be removed and cut down if the action is to be lowered. If the action is too low, shims must be used beneath the saddle or the saddle replaced if large adjustments have to be made. Tune up and test the action both by playing and by measuring string clearances at the twelfth fret. Since you want to try to get the action set correctly on the first attempt the best procedure is to first measure the present action. Then, by estimating the action you want (use the *Actions* chart as an aid), calculate the difference to find how much up or down the saddle must go. For example, if you want a height of 4 on the first string, twelfth fret, and you have measured a height of 5, you will need to lower the saddle by two sixty-fourths at the saddle. If

you have a height of 6 on the fifth string and you want to raise it to 6-1/2, you will have raise the saddle by one sixty-fourth. Yes, you guessed it already: each increment of height change at the twelfth fret requires double the change at the saddle.

To lower the saddle use a file to get to the correct height and profile and clean up with fine sandpaper. To raise the saddle use paper or thin plastic (or wood) shims beneath it. If it must be raised more than about a sixteenth of an inch or if it is in danger of being pulled forward out of the slot by string tension, it will have to be replaced.

Be particularly careful with action adjustments on acoustic-electric guitars with pickups built in to the saddle, for while the saddle can be cut down you don't want to go too far and have to resort to shims to bring it back up. Note that Ovation acoustic-electric guitar pickups are adjustable with shims only. Their saddle surface is just a thin shell and cannot be cut down. If your guitar has a separate pickup beneath the saddle, be sure to confine your filing to the upper (string side) surface. Many of these pickups require careful custom fitting of the mating surface between pickup and saddle in order to obtain even output, and filing on the bottom of the saddle will destroy this fit.

As with work on the trussrod and nut, you will be most successful if you measure your action carefully both before you begin and as you proceed. While this is important for all guitars, it is absolutely crucial for those that lack adjustable saddles.

PICKUPS

If you are working on an electric guitar, you must adjust its pickups after you have finished your work on the action, since any change in string height calls for a corresponding change in pickup height. Certain pickups can harm your guitar's intonation and action if they are not adjusted correctly. You will be amazed to find out how greatly pickup adjustments can affect your setup.

Start by adjusting for height below the strings. Most humbucking pickups should lie about 1/16" to 1/8" below the string when the string is fretted at the highest fret. This will give good output and tone for most humbuckers without affecting intonation. From here you can, if you choose, custom-adjust your pickups for variations in tone and output. One thing you can do is to equalize the output between them. Your neck pickup will give more volume than the bridge pickup if both are set at the same height, so if you want to equalize the output between them lower the neck pickup gradually until both have about the same output. Don't raise the bridge pickup. This can cause problems with distortion and interfere with your picking. While you can use output meters and other electronic aids to do this adjustment precisely, in reality it's a subjective thing where your ear is the best judge.

Adjusting the pickups: Adjust the pickups after setting the action but before intonating the bridge.

You might also want to adjust the loudness balance between the treble and bass strings. This simply requires lowering the pickup on either the treble or bass side, depending upon the balance you desire. Here again you should follow your ear.

Many humbucking pickups have individually adjustable pole pieces in one or both of the pickup coils. If you see a row of six adjustable screws (usually straight-slot, but also phillips-head and allen styles) protruding from the top of the pickup, you can take advantage of this feature to adjust the balance between the individual strings. For conventional playing and for jazz styles where strong string bends are never used, the pole piece for the second string should be lower than those for the first and third (wound) strings. If the third string is plain, its pole piece should be lower than that for the second string. If you bend strings a lot, the pole-piece screws should be higher under the middle strings and lower under the outer strings so that they will follow the arch of the string heights. While doing this will cost you some evenness of output, it will allow the strings to sustain much better when they are bent.

Adjusting the pole-piece screws: If you plan to play rock and roll or blues, adjust the pole-piece screw heights to follow the curve of the fingerboard.

For guitars with single-coil pickups (Stratocaster-style) the above comments generally hold true, but with a few modifications. First, because the magnets typically used in these pickups are very strong and will pull on the strings, the basic height setting must allow for more clearance between strings and pickup. A typical initial setting might be something like an 1/8" beneath the first string and 3/16" beneath the sixth string. If your clearances are much less than this you may quite likely encounter distortion and intonation problems. Such problems are also more likely to occur when you have three pickups, as on the Fender Stratocaster. And because the bass strings are influenced a lot more by magnet strength than are the treble strings, the bass side of a pickup must be kept lower than the treble side. Be prepared to experiment a bit in order to arrive at the best combination of volume, tone, and intonation. When you work on your action take the precaution of keeping the pickups low, because single-coil pickups, when too close to the strings, can cause a lot of mysterious fret buzzes no matter what you do with all of your action adjustments.

If you have active pickups the problems associated with Stratocaster-style single-coils may be absent because active pickups do not rely on strong magnets for proper tone and output. Low-impedance active pickups such as the EMG series have negligible interaction with the strings, giving you more freedom to adjust their heights to your preference.

Interestingly enough, you can change the tone of your guitar by adjusting your pickups. The closer the pickup is to the string, the more bass response you will get. The farther away the pickup, the greater the treble response. On humbucking pickups with adjustable pole-piece screws, you can emphasize the bass effect by adjusting the screws flush with the top of the pickup and raising it as close to the strings as you can without introducing distortion. For additional treble effect, raise the pole-piece screws well above the pickup body and lower the pickup away from the strings as much as you can while still maintaining a reasonable volume level. Even though changes in volume level will limit the range of adjustment, you may still be able to fine-tune the sound of your instrument without going to the expense of replacing the pickups.

As I noted above, if you get the pickups too close to the strings you will get distortion. While this may be exactly what you want from your guitar, the same factors which produce distortion (pickups very close to the strings and strong magnets) will also sometimes produce a distinct loss of sustain. As you may have guessed, the magnetic attraction between the string and the pickup's magnet is the culprit. The "dampening effect" as the pickup tries to attract the string quickly kills its vibration, and because this can be fairly subtle you should try moving the pickup a little farther away from the string if the volume seems to die away quickly.

Juggling all of the separate aspects of pickup adjustment—tone, distortion, volume, sustain—will in some cases involve compromises in deciding what is most important to your style of playing. Take your time when adjusting your pickups and check out your guitar's tone carefully each time you make a different adjustment. Finally, keep in mind that you may have to come back to your pickup adjustment again if your guitar's intonation adjustments don't fall within normal limits.

INTONATION

Setting the intonation means adjusting the bridge saddle (whenever adjustable) so that each string will play on every fret as accurately as possible within the limitations of the equal-tempered tuning system. (You will find an explanation of equal-tempered tuning in Chapter 5.) For now, we'll be concentrating on the mechanics of adjusting the guitar to play in tune, rather than the theory behind those mechanics.

Each time you fret a string you stretch it a small amount from its open (unfretted) position. The conse-

quent sharpness in pitch is compensated for by a slight excess in string length beyond the mathematically correct distance. Variables created by different action preferences and string types make it impossible for the manufacturer to set saddle position correctly for every playing situation.

To check the intonation of a string, first play its harmonic at the twelfth fret. Take note of the pitch of the string. Then play the same string by fretting it at the twelfth fret. If the intonation is correct the two pitches should match exactly. If the fretted note is higher than the harmonic, the guitar is playing sharp and the bridge saddle must be moved back (away from the fingerboard). If the fretted note is lower than the harmonic, the guitar is playing flat and the saddle must be moved forward (toward the fingerboard). Because the mechanics of checking the intonation of each string are simple, your success in improving your guitar's intonation depends entirely on your skill, your ears, and the degree of adjustability built in to your instrument.

Adjusting intonation: Adjust intonation by comparing the string fretted at the twelfth fret against the string's harmonic at the twelfth fret. Move the string saddles so that the two notes are equal in pitch (see Chapter 5 for more detail on tuning).

Non-adjustable fixed saddles

For guitars with fixed saddles, checking the intonation is about all you can do. Instruments in this category include most steel-string flattops as well as classical and flamenco guitars. For these guitars, go ahead and check the intonation for all six (or all twelve on twelve-string guitars) in the manner described above. Make a mental note of your findings. If all the strings are pretty close, with a few slightly sharp, some just right, and a few slightly flat, your guitar is behaving normally. If all the strings are playing sharp (or flat), your bridge saddle might have to be moved—an operation that you'll have to leave to the repair shop.

Don't despair, however, because there are some adjustments you can make to get better intonation with these guitars without resorting to major surgery. For example, if all your strings are playing sharp you can try lowering the action in order to reduce the distance the string is forced to stretch when it is pressed down to the fret. Conversely, if all your strings are playing flat you can raise the saddle slightly to increase the amount of stretch. Admittedly, this will compromise the action, but if your playing style can accommodate the change this is an easy way to make small changes in intonation.

A way to improve intonation without changing the action is to change string gauges. Generally, lighter strings will be more sensitive to stretching and will play sharper for a given action height than a heavier gauge of the same make. So if a string is playing flat, try using a lighter one, and if it's playing sharp, try a heavier one. Don't forget: if you make these changes, be sure to recheck your trussrod and action adjustments.

If you are blessed (or cursed) with a sensitive ear, you may also want to consider compensating the saddle in order to obtain more precise intonation, though this procedure gets away from normal setup adjustments. Compared to a standard saddle, where all strings leave the saddle at the same point, a compensated saddle is cut so that each string leaves at a different point along the saddle's width, thus optimizing the guitar's intonation.

Keep in mind though, that to be effective, compensating the saddle often requires that the saddle width be increased. In some cases, the saddle itself may have to be moved as well if the original location doesn't allow full adjustment for all strings. Consult your local guitar repairperson for advice.

Adjustable bridges

If your bridge is either partly or fully adjustable, you will have a lot more control over your guitar's intonation. Guitars with adjustable bridges include acoustic and electric archtop guitars, as well as most solidbody and hollowbody electric guitars and basses. With a few exceptions (archtop guitars, electric conversions of acoustic guitars), most electrics have six-way fully adjustable bridges. Intonation is very critical on electrics in general, and on rock-and-roll instruments in particular, since rock-and-roll string gauges are very sensitive to small changes in bridge and saddle position.

On bridges with moveable bases and a single saddle adjustable for height only (commonly found on archtop guitars), you can proceed by finding a compromise setting that allows for reasonable intonation on all strings. Typically, you will have to adjust the bridge so that the (single) saddle angles toward the fingerboard on the first string and away from the fingerboard on the sixth string. If you cannot find a setting that allows equally good intonation on all the strings, move the saddle so that all of the strings either play in tune or slightly sharp. Avoid having any of the strings intonate flat—a flat pitch is far more noticeable and objectionable to the ear than one that sounds slightly sharp.

Be aware that some saddles use a simple form of compensation by incorporating a "setback" on the second (B) string, in which the saddle is notched so that the second string is slightly longer than the adjacent first and third (G) strings. (Check the saddle to make sure that the setback is under the second string and not the fifth string!) This setback arrangement works well only when you use a conventional string set with a wound third string. If you use a rock-and-roll set with a plain third string, that string's intonation will be very sharp. In such a case you will be better off with a straight saddle unless you go to a custom compensated saddle such as described earlier.

For guitars with adjustable saddles the standard procedure is to check the intonation of one string, move the saddle, and check the intonation again. This may require several adjustments back and forth until you get it right, but it's easily done on most guitars. Repeat for all of the other strings.

Rock-and-roll intonation: Adjust for proper intonation last. While the saddle positions on this guitar are typical for a rock-and-roll setup, every guitar will require individual adjustment depending on design, string type, and action.

Bear in mind that you can achieve accurate intonation only when you reproduce actual playing conditions as closely as possible. As you did with the previous setup adjustments, adjust and check the intonation while holding the instrument in playing position. When fretting a string, be careful to press it straight down with no more than normal pressure.

Whether you have an electric or acoustic guitar, you can make life easier on yourself by getting an electronic guitar tuner. In particular, small errors in pitch which may go unnoticed on an acoustic guitar seem magnified on an electric. These small differences are hard to detect by ear and even harder to determine consistently. Your ears really do get "tired" after listening to the same note(s) over and over again!

Even though a tuner can, for most people, indicate smaller increments of pitch, your ear is really the judge of whether your instrument sounds in tune or not. In the end, what sounds in tune may not agree exactly with the strobe anyway. What sounds good to most people is a subtle sharpening of pitch as you go up to the higher notes. Try strobing the first and second strings slightly sharp. A couple of cents should be enough (one cent equals a hundredth of a semitone). The idea is to gradually sharpen the upper notes a small amount compared to the lower strings. This difference can't be distinguished by ear as being out of tune or tuned sharp, but it should sound "better" and "brighter." For additional details regarding guitar tuning, refer to Chapter 5.

SOME FINAL OBSERVATIONS

Now that you have finished the basic adjustments on your instrument, go ahead and do it all over again. That's right, redo all of your adjustments, but this time go over all of your settings and check to see how they work together as a whole. You might want to adjust the action on one string, or tweak the trussrod a bit to favor a certain area of the fingerboard, or adjust the height of a pickup slightly. All of these fine-tuning adjustments will of course affect the others as well, but at this stage the effect will be minimal. You don't have to go through the complete routine in strict order.

You should now have a guitar that plays well and that incorporates your preferences. But what if you have problems? What can you do about worn frets, fret buzzes that won't go away, strings that still don't play in tune regardless of gauge or age? At some point you will encounter these problems, and others, where trouble spots persist regardless of your efforts. In subsequent chapters I will cover every one of these situations. By the time you have read through this book, you will recognize which situations fall under the category of "adjustments," and which fall under the category of "repairs."

Setting up your own guitar is a challenge because of the many variables that require your analysis and judgment. But when the results of your work give you an instrument that plays and sounds better than it ever did before, that's a nice reward for your efforts. And you know you can do even better on the next one.

2
Setup Tips for Specific Models

In this chapter we'll take a look at some popular guitars and basses and examine their features. All of these models are well known. Each has idiosyncracies and requirements that demand special attention. We will use them to illustrate setup methods, tricks, and shortcuts in a practical context. Many of these tips can be carried over to similar models within the same maker's line. They can also be helpful in setting up instruments that use similar construction styles (copies, for instance). By reading through this section and using the applicable instructions when working with your instruments, you can get a good idea of what is involved in adjusting just about any electric guitar.

Fender Guitars

Many of the most popular electric guitars available today are based on a construction style in which the neck is manufactured as a separate unit and fastened onto the body with bolt and a neckplate. Pioneered by Fender, this bolt-on neck style makes setups easier to do because the neck angle can be easily changed, in contrast to the conventional construction technique of gluing the neck onto the body. It is as easy to exchange the major components (necks and bodies) on these Fender-style guitars as it is to do so with hardware like bridges, nuts, electronics, and machines.

Of the many Fender instruments available, the Stratocaster and Telecaster guitars, and the Precision and Jazz basses, because of their popularity and their many imitators, are must examples for learning electric guitar setup. Even within these four models, many variations have been made over the years, covering virtually every component. We will look at the models that have been made in the largest numbers and that you are most likely to see.

Stratocaster

The basic Stratocaster has a bolt-on neck with a 25-1/2" scale length and an adjustable trussrod, a 7-9" radius curvature on the fingerboard, three single-coil pickups with a three-way or five-way selector switch, one volume and two tone controls, and (usually) a tremolo-style bridge.

Fender Stratocaster

Trussrod: The Strat neck's trussrod, depending on the model, is accessed through the end of the neck or at the peghead. All of the original necks as well as certain current models are adjusted with a large flat-blade screwdriver. Though you might be able to work a screwdriver in at an angle without taking the neck off, it's safest to loosen the neck screws and push the neck upwards in order to adjust the rod. Other Stratocaster trussrods are adjusted with allen wrenches at the peghead. The "bullet" style takes an 1/8" allen, while others, inset beneath the nut, take a 3/16" allen.

Other Strats have a two-way adjustable rod that can be adjusted either against the pull of the strings (the usual way), or with the pull of the strings. The ability to counteract a back-bow in the neck becomes important in those situations where string tension alone is not enough to pull the neck up enough to get proper relief. Necks with the two-way rod are adjustable with a 1/8" allen wrench at the peghead end. The trussrod nut is recessed out of view and the allen wrench must be inserted through the hole in the dark wood plug directly behind the nut. Turn the wrench clockwise (viewing from the peghead) to tighten, and counter-clockwise to loosen. All Fender trussrods work effectively, so you shouldn't have any problems.

Fingerboard radius: When setting up the action bear in mind that all of the earliest Strats as well as some of the current vintage models have fingerboards with a short radius. For string bends on these necks, the first (and sometimes the second) strings will have to be relatively high off the fingerboard in order to avoid fretting out. Many of the current Strats and Strat-style guitars have larger-radius fingerboards that allow for bending with a lower action. Keep this in mind when comparing different makes and models of guitars.

Neck adjustments: Most Strats have a four-bolt neck pattern (in which the neck is held onto the body with four screws), while others have a three-bolt pattern. The four-bolt style is more stable than the three-bolt and is less prone to having the neck knocked out of alignment. If neck alignment seems to get bumped out of adjustment too easily, check the mating surfaces between the neck and body to be sure that they are both level. If shims are necessary to adjust the neck angle, keep them to a minimum so that as much contact as possible is maintained between the neck and body.

On some three-bolt and four-bolt necks Fender uses a neck angle adjuster called the Micro-Tilt system. An allen screw adjuster bears against a small plate embedded in the end of the neck. Small adjustments in neck angle can be made easily even when the strings are under tension. Just loosen the neck screws slightly, turn the allen wrench (3/32") a half turn in the desired direction, and retighten the neck screws. Repeat this procedure as many times as necessary to dial in the right angle. But while neck angle adjustments can be made in this way in just a fraction of the time it takes to adjust with shims, you may find that neck alignment is not as secure because there is less contact between the neck and body. If you find that necks with the Micro-Tilt system will not stay in line (this is more of a prob-

lem with three-bolt necks), it is perfectly permissible to use the shims instead. Or try this trick: on both three-bolt and four-bolt necks you can insert a small piece of window screen in the bolt area between the neck and body to increase friction between them.

String retainers: At the peghead all Stratocasters have a string retainer on the first and second strings to ensure proper downward tension (and maximum sustain) on the strings as they go from the nut to the machines. Some Strats also have a retainer on the third and fourth strings as well. To maintain proper down tension on the strings that lack retainers, wind enough turns on the tuning machine of each string so that the string is wound all the way down to the ferrule. This is especially important as the machines get further away from the nut, as on the third- and fourth-string machines.

Pickups: The three standard single-coil pickups on the Strat have very powerful magnets which when positioned too close to the strings will cause a wide range of problems with tone, intonation, sustain, and even fret buzz. This is especially true on the bass strings. To avoid these problems you should keep the pickups slightly lower on the bass side. You will lose a little output, but that is a necessary compromise. The amount of interaction between these single-coil pickups (the newer Lace-Sensor pickups excepted) and the overall setup is considerable, so if you change the pickup heights, recheck all of your action and intonation adjustments.

Stratocaster pickup adjustments: For best tone and intonation, the bass side of the pickups must be lowered so that the magnets will not interfere with string vibration.

Tremolo bridge: The standard Strat tremolo bridge has adjustments for individual string height and intonation as well as for tremolo-spring tension and bridge rest position. The first thing to decide is whether or not you plan to use the tremolo. If the answer is yes you have to decide either to allow the bridge to float or to use it for lowering pitch only. Because string height will change when the tremolo is employed, it is best to set the tremolo and bridge rest position before going on to action and intonation adjustments.

Regardless of how the tremolo will be used, the six screws around which the bridge pivots must not bind or hinder the movement of the bridge plate. With the bridge plate flat on the top of the guitar, check for clearance between the top of the bridge plate and the bottom of each screw head and readjust if there is no space. If the tremolo is to be used, tilt the bridge up with the tremolo arm and check the clearance again. You may have to readjust the screws again in order to keep the bridge from binding when the tremolo is being used. Overtightening the screws will cause the bridge to stick "up" and prevent the plate from returning flat onto the top.

Tremolo bridge springs: Stratocaster tremolo-style bridges use springs, fastened onto an adjustable claw to counter string tension. Most installations with rock-and-roll strings use three springs. You normally wouldn't use the maximum (five) unless you want to lock the bridge down.

The advantage of a downward-only tremolo is that the strings will stay much better in tune in the rest position because the bridge plate will stay firmly in place even with minor changes in string tension. If you need to use the tremolo to raise as well as lower the pitch of the strings, loosen the spring claw or remove a spring or two so that in rest position (be sure to keep the guitar tuned exactly to pitch) the back edge of the bridge plate will be slightly off the top. The amount of clearance will be determined by the amount you want to raise the pitch with the tremolo. As with the downward-only trem adjustment, the number of springs and the tension on the springs will affect the stiffness or softness of the tremolo action.

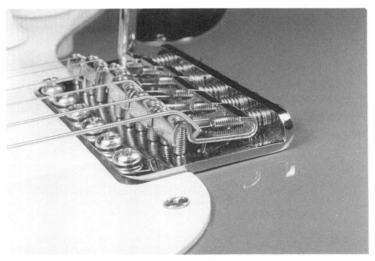

The bridge pivot screws: Be sure that the six pivot screws have enough clearance beneath the heads to allow free movement of the bridge when the tremolo is used.

If you plan to use the tremolo to lower pitch only, adjust the bridge springs so that the bridge plate lies flat on the top when the strings are at normal pitch. Depending upon the gauge of the strings you will have to adjust the number of tremolo springs (start with three) and the position of the spring claw in the body. Generally, the heavier the spring tension, the more stable the tuning will be. On the other hand, the feel of the tremolo will change depending upon the number of springs and how much they are stretched. Three springs stretched tightly can hold the bridge as tightly to the top as five springs stretched loosely, but will have a softer feel when the tremolo is used.

The basic Strat with the traditional bridge, nut, and machines, cannot be expected to stay as well in tune as the models with locking bridges and nuts. Nevertheless, there are some things you can do to improve tuning stability. If you really don't plan to use the trem, lock the bridge in place by putting all five springs in, adjust the spring claw so that the springs are stretched tight, and put in wood spacer blocks on both sides of the tremolo bridge block so that all bridge movement is prevented. You may even find that sustain is improved. Second best for stability is to use downward-only tremolo. Since the bridge doesn't float, rest-position stability at the bridge will be very good. Overall tuning stability is determined largely by the nut, string guides, and tuning machines. Try to minimize friction in these areas by making sure the strings slide smoothly through the notches in the nut and by limiting the down angle of the string to the machines. For example, use string guides with rollers (only on the first and second strings) and wrap just enough of the string onto the machine roller to maintain contact with the nut for good sustain, but not so much that excess friction is introduced, hampering smooth movement of the string through the nut.

If you will be using the trem for both upward and downward pitch changes, friction in the moving parts of the bridge-pivot screws and springs will further limit the ability of the strings to return to exact pitch. You can try to overcome the effects of friction by using extra springs, though this will stiffen the tremolo. Or you can try to reduce friction by taking out some of the inner pivot screws and by thinning out the edge of the hole that the pivot screw goes through. An accessory tremolo spring called a Trem-Setter can also help.

Of course, modifying your Strat with a locking nut and bridge would be the best solution if you plan to use the tremolo a lot, but if you have an instrument with any vintage pretensions at all it would be best to leave it stock and get a non-vintage guitar to modify, or get a guitar with all the locking stuff built in.

While most Stratocasters have tremolo bridges of the original style, others have fixed bridges. Some Strats use cast metal saddles instead of stamped metal ones, or bridge base plates of varying configurations with or without integral tremolo blocks. Some bridges pivot on knife edges and have fine tuners, while others, such as the System (I,II,III) series and the Fre-Flyte bridges, use an entirely different spring system that requires removal of the pickguard for some of the tremolo adjustments. And finally, some stock Strats use Kahler or Floyd Rose tremolos. All of this adds up to a daunting array of variations, but in reality you will mostly be working on variations of the standard tremolo bridge or one or another of the Floyd Rose-style locking bridges.

Saddle height: Set the saddle height for each string so that there is a smooth (upward) progression in from the first string to the sixth. Most actions will call for only one or two sixty-fourths of an inch difference in height between the highest and lowest strings, so be sure to measure every string for exactness. Adjust the saddles so that they are parallel with the bridge plate, and retune after every adjustment so that movement of the bridge plate, if your tremolo floats, won't interfere with the individual action adjustment.

Finish by intonating the guitar. With some string and action combinations the third- and sixth-string saddles may have to be moved close to the back of the bridge

plate. You may have to cut the bridge spring (which goes over the intonation adjustment screw) or remove it altogether in order to allow for enough movement of the saddle.

Finally, recheck all of your adjustments and listen carefully to the tone quality of the guitar as well as the accuracy of its intonation. This is an important final step with any guitar, and it is especially important with Strats because of the effect of the three single-coil pickups on all aspects of the setup.

Nut: Besides the standard bone or plastic nuts, Strats can come with locking nuts of the Floyd Rose or Kahler varieties, with several variations of the Wilkinson roller nuts, or with a locking nut of Fender design in which a thumb lever (cam arm) locks all of the strings at one time. If you have a guitar with one of these cam-arm locking nuts be very careful not to lock the arm too tightly. It's all too easy to overtighten it and snap off the locking shaft.

If you have a roller nut, such as on the Strat Plus, you risk losing a substantial amount of sustain on the open strings and encountering an annoying buzz if the string diameters do not match the slots in the nut exactly. You may have to look for a matching roller nut (they come in several slot sizes to match the usual rock-and-roll gauges) or you may need to try different gauges of strings.

Roller nut: A Strat Plus with the Wilkinson roller nut. Roller bearings in the nut minimize friction. Note the use of the locking machine, eliminating potential for tuning problems caused by multiple string wraps around the post. For best sustain, match the string gauges to the slots in the nut. This model has the Bi-Flex two-way trussrod.

Electronics: Electronic variations on some Strat models include humbucking pickups and a variety of control variations both with and without active circuitry. The standard configuration with one volume control and two tone controls is the most widely used. This is teamed together with a three-way selector (original style, with one pickup on at a time) or five-way selector (the same basic switch but with a detent in the in-between positions, allowing front and middle or middle and rear combinations of pickups in addition to the usual front, middle, and rear). Keep in mind that there is no tone control for the bridge pickup. Also, some models don't have a ground wire running between the controls and rely on a sheet of foil beneath the pickguard to supply the ground connection. If this is the case with your Strat, be sure to keep the controls tightened to the pickguard to avoid intermittent output or even a total loss of signal.

Many of the suggestions for the Stratocaster can be applied directly to Strat copies. While it isn't possible to cover every single variation of every Strat in detail, much less the copies, the basics outlined above should get you started on the right foot. There's a lot of interesting stuff going on out there with Stratocaster and Stratocaster-like guitars, and a person could easily make a specialty of repairing and restoring this one model alone. Maybe someone is already doing it.

Telecaster

One of Fender's most popular guitars, the Telecaster in its basic form features a bolt-on neck with 25-1/2" scale fingerboard, a solid body with two single-coil pickups, a non-tremolo bridge, a pickup selector switch, and single tone and volume controls. Like the Stratocaster, the Telecaster has undergone many changes in configuration, with models featuring variations in bridges, pickups, controls, and body styles. The original "vintage" model remains the most popular and it is this basic configuration which will be discussed here.

Fender Telecaster

Neck: All of the comments regarding Stratocaster necks apply equally to the Tele, so there won't be any surprises here. Remember that the small radius fingerboards on the early Fender guitars limit the amount that the strings can be bent unless the action is raised slightly.

Pickups: Both pickups on the basic Telecaster are of single-coil design, with the bridge pickup responsible for the famous Telecaster sound. In addition to this pickup's distinctive tone, it is much louder than the neck pickup. Though the pole-piece magnets are, like the Strat's, very strong and some precautions must be taken not to adjust them too close to the strings, the problems associated with having the pickup too close to the strings are not nearly as troublesome as on the Strat.

Except for some very early Teles in which the pickup selector adds an extra tone capacitor across the neck pickup in the forward switch position, the normal switch configuration is: neck pickup, both pickups, bridge pickup. The volume and tone controls both work on both pickups.

There are three height adjustment screws for the bridge pickup. The ones at either end adjust its overall height, while another in the middle allows you to adjust the pickup parallel with the strings. The screws go into a metal shielding plate below the pickup, and if you lower the pickup too much it will drop down and you will have to remove the bridge in order to reattach it. (Don't forget to include the spring that goes between the pickup base and the bridge plate.)

The neck pickup, though of single-coil design, is relatively mellow and has a considerably lower output than the bridge pickup. Its magnets are not especially strong either, so you can adjust it fairly close to the strings without affecting tone or intonation. On most Teles it is mounted to the body, with its height adjusting screws hidden beneath the pickguard, meaning that you will have to remove it if you want to get to them. On some other Teles it is mounted to the pickguard with the height adjustment screws easily accessible.

A few relatively rare Telecaster models feature one or two humbucking pickups. The pole-piece adjusting screws visible on the tops of these pickups are offset and are adjustable for volume just like the Gibson-style humbuckers. In addition, the Fender humbuckers have six more pole-piece screws on their undersides. For best effect these should be adjusted along with the upper screws.

Fender Telecaster Thinline: This model has two Fender humbucking pickups.

Bridge: Telecasters are available today with both six-way and three-way adjustable bridges, although most of the early examples have only the three-way bridge, in which each saddle serves a pair of strings. Though string height on these bridges can be adjusted easily, intonation will be a compromise between the requirements of the two strings on the saddle. It is, however, possible to achieve near-perfect intonation on a three-way bridge by bending each intonation-adjusting screw so that the saddle skews from side to side as the screw is turned. The amount of bend in the screw determines the angle of the saddle to the strings (and therefore the precise amount of compensation), permitting, with a little experimentation, very accurate intonation for all strings. Six-way adjustable bridges, of course, can be adjusted without your having to resort to "tricks" like this.

Telecaster bridge: It's possible to get six-way adjustment out of a three-way bridge. This bridge is adjusted for rock-and-roll strings, with a plain third string.

FENDER BASSES

Fender's Precision and Jazz basses have set the standard for electric basses for many years. Because of their popularity and because of the many instruments inspired by them (and copied from them), their setup requirements are worth examining.

Precision Bass

The typical Precision Bass comes with a 34" scale bolt-on neck with an adjustable trussrod, twenty frets, and a rosewood or lacquered maple fingerboard. The P-Bass features a solid body with a single split pickup, single volume and tone controls, and a fully adjustable bridge. As with other Fender instruments, the Precision Bass has been offered with many variations like active electronics, different bridge styles, and varying pickup combinations. Some models feature an additional Jazz Bass pickup in the bridge position.

Fender Precision Bass

Fender P/Jazz Bass: This Fender bass has both Jazz- and Precision-style pickups. This model features Lace Sensor pickups and a fine-tuning bridge.

Neck: All of the early P-Bass necks as well as the current reissues have trussrods adjustable with a large screwdriver at the base of the neck. The adjustment nut is partially exposed when the neck is bolted onto the body, but it is usually best to unscrew the four neck mounting screws (or three, as on some models) and push the neck upwards in order to gain unobstructed access. Other trussrod types are adjustable with an allen wrench at the peghead. As on the Fender guitar necks, shims are sometimes called for when the neck angle does not fall within the adjustment range of the bridge.

Because electric basses have long necks and high string tension relative to electric guitars, sometimes the necks flex more than the trussrod can handle. This is especially critical at the base of the neck beyond the twelfth fret and at the nut area around the first and second frets. Check this out carefully when adjusting the trussrod, because even though Fender bass necks have better trussrods than most, it is very hard to get proper relief throughout the length of the neck when problems occur in these areas. Fender bass necks (like most) will flex substantially with and without string tension. Don't be surprised if the neck bends up an eighth of an inch or more under string tension.

Pickup: The split pickup on the P-Bass is actually composed of two single-coil pickups, with each pickup handling the output from two strings. They are wired in series and, importantly, they are not interchangeable even though they look identical. Fender calls the unit for the third and fourth strings the "rhythm" pickup and the unit for the first and second strings the "lead" pickup. Because the two pickups, when wired correctly, are really a single humbucking pickup in disguise, you should have them checked out if you are having problems with hum or with poor tone.

Adjust the pickups for good output without getting them too close to the strings. A good starting point is 1/8" below the strings held down at the highest fret.

Precision Bass pickups: Adjust them so that they are about 1/8" below the strings. Note that the angle of the pickups follows the radius of the fingerboard.

Bridge: Though details have varied throughout the years, all Precision Basses (except for the very early models, which had only one saddle per pair) have individually adjustable saddles for each string, making intonation adjustments straightforward. If the saddle height adjustment screws are at either end of their adjustment range, it would be best to readjust the neck angle. Though in recent years I haven't heard much about the problem, in the past the adjustment screws on Fender basses would sometimes unscrew themselves because of vibration from the strings. Some players would have to raise the saddles once or twice in an evening if they didn't want to end up with an ultra-low action. If this is happening to you, try painting a little lacquer on the threads (as Fender did), or apply a little glue such as Lok-Tite.

Most players remove the finger-rests and the bridge and pickup covers from their P-Basses. Some bridge covers have a sponge-rubber mute hidden inside, so if your bass has a cover and your tone lacks brightness and sustain…

Jazz Bass

The Jazz Bass, another popular model from Fender, offers more tone variations than the Precision because of its double-pickup configuration. With two single-coil pickups, a volume control for each pickup and a single tone control for both (early models had "stacked pots" with concentric volume and tone controls for each pickup), a solid body, and a fully adjustable bridge, the Jazz model has a sound distinctly different from the other basses in the Fender line.

Fender Jazz Bass

Neck: Jazz Basses come with a 34" scale bolt-on neck with specs similar to that of the Precision. The necks are typically narrower in width at the nut (several widths have been available), and many J-Basses have bound fingerboards with block position markers. All of the observations and precautions covered with the Precision Bass apply equally to the Jazz. In fact, J-Bass necks, because they are usually narrower at the nut than those on P-Basses, have the potential for more problems with uncontrolled neck flex.

The fretless versions of the Jazz and Precision necks have no fret slots at all, as opposed to fretless conversions featuring either a contrasting wood inlay in the fret slot or the original fret tang (after the fret crown has been ground off). Use the same criteria for judging a fretless neck as you would with a fretted neck. When leveling the fingerboard (the equivalent of doing a fretmill) use sandpaper attached to a straight sanding block around ten inches long. If anything, leveling a fingerboard is more critical than milling frets because the opportunities for string buzzes on a fretless finger-

board are infinite. And even though you can vary intonation with your fingers on a fretless bass, take as much trouble intonating the bridge saddles as on a fretted instrument. You will be rewarded with consistent fingering all over the fingerboard.

Pickups: Each pickup on a Jazz Bass can be adjusted for volume independently. When both pickups are full on they give a humbucking effect. For this reason they are not interchangeable, and their polarity must be respected if the wiring is changed. In any event, the bridge pickup is slightly longer than the neck pickup. As with the P-Bass pickup, adjust them so that they are about an eighth of an inch away from the string when it is fretted at the highest fret. Incidentally, the pickups on both the Precision and the Jazz are mounted on top of foam rubber; the foam may require replacement if it can't hold the pickups snug up against the height adjustment screws. The pickups should be close enough for good volume but not so close that you might strike them while playing.

Fender Jazz Bass pickups: Adjust them about 1/8" away from and level with the strings.

Bridge: The bridge on the Jazz Bass is identical to that of the Precision (watch out for that mute inside the bridge cover). All adjustments and precautions are the same.

From a setup standpoint, Fender's Jazz and Precision basses are satisfying to work on because all their components are readily adjustable and easy to get to. Pay special attention to the neck setup and/or fretmill, for the neck on an electric bass is its most critical component.

GIBSON GUITARS

Les Paul

One of the most famous guitars of all time, the Les Paul has been around since the early fifties. Despite the many variations that have come and gone over the years, most of the basic construction features on today's models are remarkably similar to those on the very first examples. The basic Les Paul features a solid body of maple and Honduras mahogany, a glued-on mahogany neck, a rosewood or ebony fingerboard, a 24-3/4" scale length, two humbucking pickups with a toggle selector switch, and individual volume and tone controls.

Gibson Les Paul Custom

Within the original theme, just about every component affecting tone has been changed at one time or another, including the tailpiece and bridge, the pickups and controls, and the wood varieties used in the body and neck. Moreover, entirely different models—the Specials, Juniors, SG body styles, and low-impedance Recording—have been spun off from the original Les Paul. While some of these are interesting to examine, especially the low-impedance version, the models that best represent the Les Paul lineup and will be discussed here are the Les Paul Standard, Custom, and Deluxe. These three share the same body design, and really only differ in cosmetics (binding, finishes, fretwire sizes) and pickup variations (small humbuckers on the Deluxe and three pickups on some of the Customs). Since they have basically the same construction and hardware, they require the same kind of setup and action work. In fact, other models in the Gibson line that feature similar parts and construction, like the Explorer, Firebird, SG, and Flying V, can be set up using similar methods.

Neck: Les Paul necks are glued onto the body with a mortise-and-tenon joint that runs from the end of the fingerboard to where the neck joins the body. Such a large gluing surface ensures a sure attachment; rare is the neck that comes loose or that needs to have its angle changed. Still, when you examine a neck for straightness, take special care to check the fingerboard from the twelfth fret to its upper limit. Since the trussrod is not effective in this area, any deviation in straightness—especially an upturn, or "ski jump"—can pose serious problems not remediable by setup adjustments alone. Even a fretmill may not be enough. Problems of this sort usually require removal of the frets, leveling of the fingerboard, and a refretting.

In all other respects the necks on Les Pauls are easily adjustable and should pose no problems whatsoever. If your neck hasn't been adjusted recently, however, it would be wise to remove the trussrod nut completely (use a 5/16" nutdriver) and put a drop of oil on the threads before making any major changes in tension. Gibson trussrods are strong enough to withstand any normal tension, but rust can form on their threads under damp conditions, freezing up the nut and introducing the potential for breakage of the rod at that point. Trussrods can be repaired (sometimes quite easily and without disturbing the fingerboard), but why take a chance? Take a minute to lubricate the threads and be safe.

Although jumbo fretwire has been used on most Les Pauls in recent years, many of the earlier models had medium wire, while some of the Customs had "fretless wonder" fretwire. It looked like heavily milled mandolin wire and represented Gibson's approach at the time (fifties to seventies) to achieving a fast action. Most Custom owners went directly from the store to the repair shop to have their guitars refretted with jumbo wire. Unlike this failed experiment, normal medium and jumbo fretwire can be milled a number of times before having to be replaced.

The radius of the Les Paul fingerboard is twelve inches. Unlike the original Fenders, which have a seven-and-a-half inch radius, you can easily do string bends without having to raise the action if the fingerboard beyond the twelfth fret does not rise excessively. With a neck in reasonable condition you should have no problems adjusting the action.

Bridge: Most Les Pauls have the ABR1 Tune-O-Matic bridge or a newer variation called the Nashville Tune-O-Matic, made by Schaller. Both work well, with our nod going to the Nashville version because of its superior range of adjustability and its quietness with respect to mechanical noise. The original Tune-O-Matic doesn't have a retainer wire to hold the saddles in place, so that if a string breaks there is a good possibility of the saddle falling out and getting lost. On updated ABR1s the retainer tends to make a loose fit and will rattle or touch the vibrating string if you are careless with the bridge setup.

On both bridges the saddle-adjusting screw heads should face the rear pickup. While there is nothing wrong with having them face the tailpiece, you will get better screwdriver access to the adjusters with the screws facing forward. Gibsons fitted with Bigsby or Vibrola tailpieces make an exception to this rule. Here the screw heads should face back toward the tailpiece to eliminate the chance of them working themselves upwards to touch the vibrating string when the vibrato is used. Tapered thumbwheels are used whenever a vibrato tailpiece is installed so that the bridge can rock back and forth with the motion of the strings.

Because of the limited saddle adjustment range of the ABR1, certain string and action combinations may require that the tapered part of the saddle face back on some strings and forward on others. Normally, with a rock-and-roll set the saddles on the plain third string and the sixth string must angle back toward the tailpiece, while the others face forward. You can easily do this yourself without any tools except a small screwdriver to turn the saddle screw. The saddles on the Nashville bridge can also be turned around, though it will be a little more time-consuming than with the ABR1 because the screw retainer (or circlip) takes more time to remove and replace. In any event, this usually doesn't have to be done on the Nashville bridge on account of the longer range of travel of each of its saddles.

Replacement Tune-O-Matic bridge saddles don't have any string slots, so you will have to cut them yourself. This takes a little time, but it does give you a chance to get exactly the string spacing you want. You will have to notch or renotch the saddles anyway, because while some arch is built into the bridge, final setting of individual string heights must be done by adjusting saddle-groove depth. Use the same files and saws that you used to fit the nut (see Chapter 1), and angle the notches back toward the tailpiece so that the strings will get firm contact on the front edge of the saddle.

Middle strings much lower than the outside ones are usually an indication that the bridge base has collapsed in the middle (giving a sway-backed appearance when viewed from the ends) and needs to be straightened before adjustments on the individual saddles will do any good. Take the bridge out and place blocks on its upper ends and on the lower middle of its base. Now place the bridge base in a strong vise and *slowly* close the vise to bend the bridge back into its original shape. This problem normally occurs only on the original Tune-O-Matic and not the Nashville, but it's best to check anyway.

The stop tailpiece on the Les Paul is set so that there will be good down tension on the strings behind the bridge. Normally, this means that the tailpiece is not screwed down tight to the top. While people have claimed that adjusting the stop tailpiece down to the top increases sustain, you will have to determine for yourself whether or not this will work for your own playing situation. There is no denying the fact that excessive down tension can lead to premature bending of the bridge base as well as premature breakage of strings.

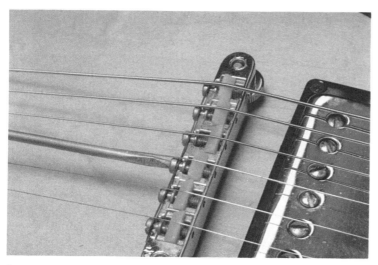

Intonating the Tune-O-Matic bridge: For proper intonation the saddle will have to angle back toward the tailpiece when the third string is plain. This usually has to be done for the sixth string, and sometimes the fifth as well.

Gibson Les Paul bridge and pickups: The stop tailpiece should be lowered only enough to ensure good down tension on the strings. The tapered pickup rings help keep the pickups parallel to the strings.

Pickups: Gibson's well-known humbucking pickups can be adjusted very close to the strings without adverse effect on the intonation or tone. When held down at the highest fret the strings should clear the pickups by 1/16" to 1/8". The main consideration is to keep them far enough away from the strings that your fingers or pick will not hit them. In addition to the noise that will be reproduced through the amplifier if this happens, mechanical abuse can damage the pickups. This is especially true when the pickup covers have been removed.

If your pickups have been "hot-rodded" (original magnets replaced with stronger ones), or replaced with high-output models, check carefully for effects on intonation. Both intonation and sustain can suffer when "hot" pickups are too close to the strings. Keep in mind the different ways you can adjust the pickup and the pole-piece screws to bring out different shadings of tone.

Electronics: Most Les Paul models use the standard Gibson two volume and two tone controls and three-way toggle selector switches. The toggle switch selects bridge or neck pickup in the outside positions and both pickups in the center position. When both pickups are in the circuit, there is normally a slight decrease in output and a slight drop in bass response when both volume controls are in the full-on position. When both pickups are in the circuit, turning one volume control completely off shuts off output for the other pickup.

Owners of the three-pickup Les Paul Custom (and certain other three-pickup Gibsons, including some SG Customs and Firebirds) should be aware that the middle switch position connects the middle pickup to the bridge pickup. Both bridge and middle pickup feed into the bridge pickup's volume and tone control.

Other Les Paul models

Although the Standard, Deluxe, and Custom models have been the most popular Les Pauls, sharing features and parts common to many Gibson electrics, others deserve mention because of their long production histories.

The original so-called "gold top" Les Paul is rarely seen today. It has single-coil P-90 pickups and an "under"-style trapeze tailpiece bridge with limited adjustability. Though many of these guitars have been converted in the past to stop-tailpiece and Tune-O-Matic bridge combinations, the existing original examples should be left stock for collectors. A later variation of the gold top has a stop-tailpiece bridge and is easier to play, though it too has primitive intonation adjustability. The Badass conversion for Gibsons with stop-tailpiece bridges offers individually adjustable saddles and has been a popular conversion for several Les Paul and SG models.

Les Paul Juniors and Specials are economy solidbody guitars with one or two P-90 pickups and stop-tailpiece bridges. A Badass bridge conversion (or Schaller equivalent) is a must if these guitars are to play anywhere near in tune. P-90 pickups have a nice warm tone, though they are noisier than humbuckers because of their single-coil design. They continued to be used well after the humbucking design became popular. Though their pole-piece screws can be individually adjusted as on the humbucking pickups, their height is not easily adjustable except with shims.

Among the most interesting of the Les Paul guitars, the low-impedance pickup Recording models and Triumph basses featured advanced passive circuitry, considering when they were created. They were designed to be plugged directly into a studio board and consequently lack a high-impedance jack. One version even has an XLR jack in the upper bout so that a microphone can be plugged in. While a line transformer can be retrofitted, these guitars still don't have the typical Les Paul sound. They have never been very popular.

The SG-style Les Paul model of the early sixties has a mahogany body of the SG style, much thinner than a usual Les Paul, with a flat top and back, contoured sides, and a double cutaway. In common with SGs, most of the neck on the SG Les Paul is clear of the body. Because the routing for the neck pickup doesn't leave much wood to hold the neck onto the body, this area is pretty fragile and won't take much abuse. Otherwise this model works pretty much like a normal Les Paul.

ES335

The Gibson ES335 series is typical of the semi-hollowbody style of guitar. It is very shallow, with a laminated, arched top and back. The ES335 features a double cutaway and a neck joined to the body at the nineteenth fret. A solid section running the full length of the body joins the top and back, while hollow "wings" form its upper and lower bouts. The pickups, bridge, and tailpiece are mounted onto the solid center section, while the controls are mounted in the lower bout. The solid section helps to dampen feedback, while the body resonates just enough to give a tone warmer than that of the typical solidbody.

Gibson ES-335

The similar-looking ES330 lacks the solid center section, and as a consequence this guitar (and others like it) will feed back much more readily than the ES335. Since a hollow body allows for more vibration of the top and back, the ES330 has a warmer tone but lacks the sustain of the ES335. Other guitars in the ES335 series include the ES340, ES345, and ES355, as well as the Epiphone equivalents made by Gibson. As with the Les Paul series of guitars, many of the differences among models in the 335 series lie in the cosmetics, such as binding, body colors, metal plating, and wood selection. All the guitars in the 335 series have two humbucking pickups, a three-way switch with two volume and two tone controls, a 24-3/4" fingerboard scale length, and a Tune-O-Matic bridge, making their setup routine very similar to that required for a Les Paul.

Bridge: The stop-tailpiece version is the most popular, though many 335s were produced with a trapeze tailpiece. While it is possible to convert these to the stop-tailpiece style, this operation should be done with care by a qualified person. Because the center block is not wide enough to allow much room for error, the anchors for the tailpiece studs must be lined up carefully. Though many guitars have already been converted, you may want to consider the collectible value of your guitar if it is still original.

Models with the Bigsby vibrato tailpiece are normally fitted with a Tune-O-Matic bridge having thumbwheels with a tapered upper surface, allowing the bridge to "rock" when the vibrato is used. The intonation screws should face back toward the tailpiece to prevent the screw heads from working themselves upwards and touching the vibrating strings. Don't expect the Bigsby to return exactly in tune every time.

Neck: The 335 neck is normally trouble free, and its trussrod works well, but because most of the neck is clear of the body you should check carefully for neck problems above the twelfth fret. Too much of a fingerboard upturn in the upper neck area (if it can't be adjusted) will cause action problems and will limit the amount the strings can be bent without fretting out.

Electronics: Some models of the 335 have a Vari-Tone control, a six-way switch handling a series of capacitors and chokes to give a wider range of tone possibilities than is possible with capacitors alone. Whereas a normal tone control just rolls off treble response, the Vari-Tone circuit cuts bass response at one extreme and treble response at the other. While this works pretty well, it causes the overall output to change substantially, making it necessary to adjust volume each time the switch is moved. In the present era of active circuitry such an interaction between tone and volume would be unacceptable, but in its day the Vari-Tone was "state-of-the-art" (though acceptance by the average player was less than overwhelming).

In addition to tone control variations, some models of the 335 series are wired for stereo output (any model with the letters SV following the model number). You will get only one pickup to work on a stereo model when you plug a mono cord into the output jack. To get the benefits of stereo output, you must use a stereo cord into two separate amps. To get output from both pickups without stereo, use a Y-adaptor cord or have the guitar rewired (as many have done) for mono output.

Although wiring and rewiring a guitar is not a part of setting it up, you may need to get at the wiring in order to clean the controls or to check for problems. Though wiring on the typical solidbody guitar is easy to get to, the semi-hollowbody guitar poses some problems. The main difficulty is with getting to the controls and pickups. On an ES335 you must go through the bridge pickup opening. Everything can be removed intact through this opening except for the neck pickup, which must be wired separately. There is a groundwire coming from the stud tailpiece anchor or from the trapeze tailpiece; unsolder this if it is too short to allow access to the component you want to get to.

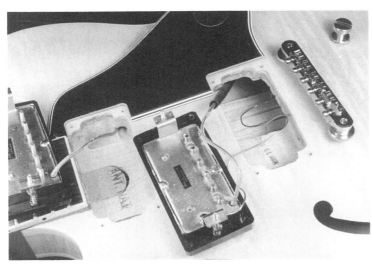

ES-335 control removal: The control harness on the Gibson ES-335 can be removed through the opening below the rear pickup. Access is tight.

Unless you have mechanical damage, a shot of contact cleaner in the controls, jack, and switch is all that will be needed to keep everything working quietly and smoothly. You can usually perform this kind of operation simply by dropping the controls down into the body and pushing them around a bit in order to allow the cleaner to be squirted in.

If you need to take the guts out, proceed carefully and don't place unnecessary strain on any of the wiring. Gibson control knobs have splined shafts, so slide them upwards to remove them. The shaft nuts and control pointers (if supplied) can then be removed and the controls pushed into the body. Don't pry with any hard tools if a knob is tight on the shaft. Instead, slip a cloth beneath the knob and wrap it around so that you can pull up on the twisted ball that holds the knob. Wiggle the cloth as you pull up and the knob should lift off easily.

Actually, getting the wiring harness out is the easy part. Getting it back in without damaging anything takes much more care. Because the jack is so far away from any openings, try attaching a wire or string to it to help guide it back into place. If you expect to be doing wiring work of the same type in the future, you can make a tool consisting of the shaft from a phone plug soldered to a long stiff wire (a coat-hanger wire will do). When you are ready to snake the wiring back into the body, insert the tool into the body through the jack hole, plug it into the jack, and pull gently as you guide the wiring harness back into place. For the other components, pushing the parts with your fingers (through the f-hole) and grasping the shafts with tweezers or long-nose pliers will do the job.

If your guitar has a Vari-Tone the procedure will be the same, but you can expect to spend a lot more time guiding the harness in and out of the body. The choke coils will have to be unscrewed from the body in order to get access, and the Vari-Tone control itself takes up a lot of room. With a little patience it can be done.

In completing the setup on your 335 (and many other Gibson models as well), take note of the pickup rings. On the 335 these are normally thin and tapered. The thick end of the ring goes toward the bridge, holding the pickup surface parallel to the strings. You may find that the neck pickup will better remain parallel to the strings if the ring is reversed, with the thick end toward the fingerboard. With all Gibsons the pole-piece screws on the pickups should face away from each other, with the neck pickup screws toward the neck and the bridge pickup screws toward the bridge.

OVATION ACOUSTIC-ELECTRICS

The Ovation line of guitars employs unconventional construction techniques and materials. Ovation's principal innovation was the use of synthetic materials to form a molded bowl to replace the wooden back and sides of the standard guitar. Ovation tops—excepting the Adamas and Elite models—are made of spruce with round soundholes. They are heavily coated with a polyurethane finish, giving the top a lot of strength as well as influencing the tone of the guitar. Ovation's top-end instruments, such as the Adamas and Elite models, use a "distributed" soundhole system, with many smaller holes in the upper bouts rather than a single soundhole. The top-of-the-line Adamas is made with a composite top of graphite and birch. All Ovation steel-string guitars use a 25-1/4" scale length fingerboard, while its nylon-string models employ a scale of 26-3/16".

Ovation Legend

Neck: The original Ovation necks were glued into the body with a dovetail joint, but current models have bolt-on style necks. The earliest models had a standard trussrod with the nut adjusted from the peghead end (1/4" hex socket). As with other guitars with peghead-adjustable trussrod nuts, the peghead is a potential weak point. Later models have the cast-aluminum Kaman Bar neck reinforcement and a trussrod nut adjustable at the endblock. It takes a 3/16" allen wrench to adjust the nut, and while the adjusting process is normal, it may take a little experimentation to connect with the nut through the soundhole. The Adamas and Elite models will require a long-handled wrench (about 10") or an allen socket with extension in order to reach the nut through the backplate.

Ovation Adamas II trussrod: The Adamas II, like other Ovations that lack a round soundhole, has an access plate in the bowl. The trussrod can be adjusted through this opening with a 3/16" allen. The opening also allows for servicing of the electronics.

Ovation Legend trussrod: The Ovation trussrods on all round-soundhole models are accessible through the soundhole. The adjusting nut is at the base of the neck, just beneath the fingerboard. Use a 3/16" allen wrench.

It is very common for the upper ends of Ovation fingerboards to drop off at the point where the neck joins the body. This is the way the guitars come from the factory and is not really a cause for concern. In any event it is certainly better than having the fingerboards turn up (ski-jump) and cause fret buzz.

Pickups and electronics: All acoustic-electric Ovations use a pickup system built into the saddle, with six individual piezo crystals potted in a silicone compound within a metal channel. The strings ride over a delrin saddle that is molded to give a small amount of compensation to aid intonation. All models (except for the Celebrity) use a preamp, with some incorporating a three-band equalizer in addition to the volume control. Be sure to unplug the cord when the instrument is not in use so that the battery will not get run down prematurely. Though the guitars which incorporate the OP-24 preamplifier (with three-band equalizer) have a battery checker built in, it would be prudent to keep a spare 9-volt battery around anyway.

If a string suddenly loses volume, you may find that the saddle has pulled away from contact with the silicone compound and piezoelectric crystals, diminishing the output or destroying it altogether. You can usually restore the sound by adding a little fresh silicone compound—the same stuff you use for caulking a bathtub—beneath the saddle and pressing the saddle back into place. Glue the edges with a little cyanoacrylate adhesive to make sure that it won't come apart again. While the earlier Ovation pickups were hardwired into the preamp, the later ones have subminiature plugs; check these if you suddenly lose all output.

Top: The finish on the Ovation top is very thick and hard, giving a lot of protection and preventing a lot of potential top cracks. On the other hand, cracks which may develop in the finish tend to be quite noticeable from certain angles and are sometimes hard to tell from cracks in the top. Top cracks should be repaired, while cracks in the finish can generally be ignored.

Action: Setting up the action on Ovation guitars is the same for all models, generally following the procedures for a standard electric guitar setup. When adjusting the saddle height, use shims of different thicknesses beneath the pickup-saddle assembly. The original shims supplied with the guitar can be used in different combinations, or, if these are missing, you can use thin hard plastic or wood shims. If the string heights for both bass side and treble side can't be adjusted properly with shims of even thickness, you will have to make some tapered shims (wood is easiest to use). Never cut or file the saddle to lower the action. The saddle surface is very thin, and once you cut into it the silicone material inside will not support the string and the electric (and acoustic) response will be altered.

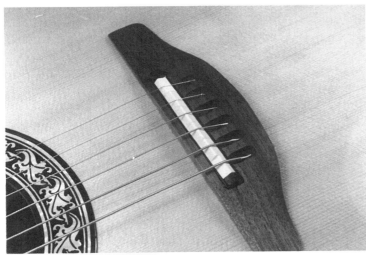

The Ovation bridge pickup: The Ovation bridge pickup uses piezo crystal sensors (potted in silicone) beneath each string. Action adjustments are done with shims; several shims are included with each new guitar.

ARCHTOP ELECTRIC GUITARS

As far as setup and action are concerned, the archtop electric guitar differs from other electric instruments in several important ways. It typically has a carved or laminated top and back and two f-holes rather than a central round soundhole (from this also comes one of its other names, the f-hole guitar). The archtop uses braces to counter string tension since it has no support block between its top and back. Its bridge, which is usually adjustable for height (and may also be adjustable for intonation), is not fastened down to the top and relies instead on string tension to hold it in place.

Pickup configurations vary. Some acoustic instruments, such as the Guild Artist Award and Gibson Johnny Smith, make use of pickups attached to the end of the neck or to the pickguard. They "float" so that they may hinder the acoustic tone as little as possible. Other instruments, like the Gibson L-5 and Super 400, begin as acoustic instruments and have pickups and controls permanently set into their tops. Still others, like the Gretsch White Falcon and the Gibson ES-775, are clearly envisioned to be electric instruments, with their tone colored by the hollowbody design. Finally, we might also include in the category certain thin hollowbody electrics, such as the Gibson Byrdland and ES-330.

Gibson L-5CES

Floating bridge: With archtop guitars the only real departure from the setup techniques we have already encountered concerns placing the floating bridge in proper position. This depends upon whether or not the bridge is supplied with a fixed wood saddle or with a Tune-O-Matic-type saddle with individual compensation for each string. For guitars with fixed wood saddles, proceed in the following manner: select the model and gauge of string you wish to use and restring the guitar. Position the bridge on the guitar so that the distance from the nut to the forward edge of the saddle at the first string will be equal to scale length (that is, twice the distance from the nut to the twelfth fret) plus 1/32" extra. To get the approximate position for the saddle on the sixth-string side add 1/8" to the scale length. Try to get the bridge position set before tuning up to pitch, as it will be harder to move the bridge when strings are under full tension. For the same reason, adjust the bridge height as much as possible before tuning to pitch.

After you have set the bridge in this initial "trial" position, go ahead with all of the usual action and setup adjustments. Your final intonation adjustments should be done last, and, because of the fixed saddle, the intonation will have to be a compromise. Don't allow any of the strings to play flat. By adjusting the overall position and angle of the bridge you should be able to get good intonation for all strings. Keep in mind, though, that because of the radically different compensation requirements between wound and plain third strings, fixed saddles work best with wound third strings. This is especially true with compensated (but not individually adjustable) wood saddles where there is a "setback" for the second string. These can be made to work well with wound third string sets (be sure that the setback is under the second string) but give very poor intonation with rock-and-roll strings containing a plain third string.

If you use rock-and-roll strings, you must have a bridge with individually adjustable string inserts in order to get acceptable intonation. On Gibson guitars the wood saddle is interchangeable with a Tune-O-Matic saddle, so this is easily accomplished. After-market archtop bridges with individually adjustable string inserts are also readily available. Adjust these bridges in the usual manner, as described in Chapter 1.

With an archtop, though, always check the bridge saddle-height adjustment to see whether or not there is any room for additional adjustment—both up and down. If the bridge is lowered as much as it can go and the action is still too high, the neck angle might have to be changed. If the bridge is adjusted to its upper limits and the action is too low, the neck angle can be bad or the top arching may have collapsed. These are expensive problems to correct, so this is one of the first things to check over. You should be especially alert for action problems caused by collapsed arching, because this defect can require disassembly of the guitar in order to reinforce, replace or reglue the tone bars that reinforce the top. If the guitar in question is an electric conversion from a pure acoustic model, check the tone bars to be sure that they weren't weakened or cut completely through when the pickups were installed. If you yourself are contemplating converting an acoustic archtop to an electric model (with the pickups built into the top), check to be sure that the arching will not be damaged or altered. As an alternative, consider a floating pickup setup, as on the Gibson Johnny Smith guitar.

Check the fit of the bridge base to the top. While this is not as critical to the tone on an electric archtop as it is on an acoustic archtop, the fit will nevertheless affect the tone. If it is really poor, damage to the top can result, and in some cases the bridge may not stay firmly in place. To improve the fit try laying a sheet of sandpaper on the top directly beneath the bridge base position and sanding the base to fit. Use a sheet of 100 grit sandpaper and determine the exact position of the bridge base by going through the setup procedure described above. Place the bridge over the sandpaper and sand in short (1/2") strokes at right angles to the direction of the strings. Be absolutely certain to keep the contact surface between the base and the top parallel so that there is no tendency for the bridge to tip when string tension is applied. The tone will also be best when maximum contact is maintained between the feet of the bridge base and the top of the guitar.

You may find that, depending upon the string gauge and action, the bridge will not stay in position when you play. This is normally not a problem except with short-scale guitars or with guitars where there is insufficient downward pressure from the strings to hold the bridge in position when you play hard. Bad alignment between the neck, bridge, and tailpiece also contributes to this situation. Some ways to hold the bridge in place include gluing small strips of sandpaper to the bridge base, gluing the bridge base (definitely not recommended!), and fastening it with small screws. If you wish to fasten the bridge permanently with screws, first check to be sure that there are no neck alignment and neck angle problems. If everything is okay, go through the normal setup and intonation adjustments and position the bridge base so that its placement can be accurately duplicated. If you have individually adjustable string inserts, leave room in your intonation work so that you can make compensation adjustments in the future without having to move the bridge base. Use two small screws to fasten the bridge base to the top, placing one below each thumbwheel so that they will not be seen. The black pickup-ring screws used on Gibson pickup rings will work well. Always drill a pilot hole for the screw and countersink the screw head.

Electronics: If you have to take out the wiring for any reason, this is usually done through the bridge pickup opening in the top (see the discussion in the ES-335 section above). The deep sides and hollow bodies of these guitars usually make for very easy access. As with semi-hollowbody guitars, most archtop electrics have a groundwire going to the tailpiece; usually it won't have to be removed when you work on the controls or wiring harness since these components can just be laid out on top of the guitar (on top of a protective cover!).

Archtop wiring access: The controls on most archtop electrics can usually be removed through the rear pickup opening. The full hollowbody style and absence of interior blocks makes access easy (compared to thin hollowbody and semi-hollow instruments).

Feedback can be a problem with archtop guitars. Controlling feedback can be as simple as using the right playing technique (some players are artists in the use and control of feedback), or reducing volume and repositioning speakers. Other measures require modification of the guitar itself; these involve reducing the acoustic resonance of the body. With the exception of the (long-since-discontinued) Van Eps string damper, a little gizmo mounted on the peghead in place of the trussrod cover, with a flip-up mute to dampen the open strings, the usual route to take is to first cover the soundholes. This helps a little on the lower feedback frequencies. The next step is to install a block beneath the bridge between the top and back. Alternatively, "soundposts" can be installed beneath each bridge foot. These will help to dampen the vibration of the top (and consequent feedback), but don't expect any of these measures to be a cure-all for all of your feedback problems. If you need to play at high volume levels, the archtop electric is probably the wrong guitar for you in the first place.

Feedback is caused by the same thing that gives the archtop guitar its full, rich tone—the vibration of the guitar's top. Since the pickups are mounted directly to the top, its vibration is transmitted to the pickups, and adding the vibration of the pickup to the original string vibration gives you a very complex output with plenty of overtones to warm up and enrich the fundamental note. Don't be surprised to find loud and weak notes as you play; the same top resonances which warm up the tone vary both in strength and in frequency.

3
ELECTRIC BASS NOTES

Setting up an electric bass is much more difficult than setting up a guitar. Adjusting basses to suit the varied requirements of contemporary players is difficult enough. Getting them to play without fret buzzes and with a range of actions approaching that of the electric guitar challenges even the professional repairperson. For someone who hasn't tried to set up a bass the above statements may seem exaggerated, but they really are true.

The neck is the most critical and troublesome part of a bass. Typically, electric basses have long scale lengths of around thirty-four inches and, following the Fender style, many have bolt-on necks and deep cutaways that leave most of the neck exposed. Affected also by the high string tension and heavy gauge strings necessary on a bass, many necks understandably behave less predictably to trussrod adjustments than do guitars.

Strings can sometimes exhibit an unevenness in diameter, and while a variation of a few thousandths of an inch is a small percentage of the overall diameter of a string, in absolute terms such variations can make buzzing on the frets very difficult to eliminate. Considering the high cost of bass strings, most people would think twice before replacing a suspected bad string—especially if it is new.

Another factor is the presence of resonant spots on certain areas on the fingerboard. These can be very pronounced on many electric basses, producing dead spots (the fifth- to seventh-fret area on Fender-style bass necks is a well-known one) and wild string vibrations that sometimes make it hard to tell whether a fret buzz is caused by an uneven fret, a bad string, or some other thing. This "voodoo factor" can make adjustment work on certain basses frustrating because nothing you do seems to have any effect on these trouble spots.

ACTION ADJUSTMENTS

Now that I've warned you about the problems that you might face when setting up your electric bass, let's meet the challenge and get specific so that you can learn to deal with them successfully.

Trussrod adjustments follow the procedures outlined for electric guitars, but because of the increased flexibility of the bass neck, a little more trial and error may be required. This is especially true when (on bolt-on necks) the trussrod nut is buried in the body at the end of the fingerboard, making it necessary to loosen the strings and partially remove the neck in order to expose it for adjustment. The bass must be put back together and tuned up after every trussrod adjustment in order to determine the straightness of the neck. Tuning to pitch is very important when working with basses because their highly flexible necks will react to the smallest changes in string tension. When checking for straightness and relief, be certain to hold the bass in normal playing position. The straightness of the neck and the tuning can vary a surprising amount when the bass is set down on a tabletop unsupported.

Sometimes a trussrod will not be able to straighten the neck in the desired area of the fingerboard or will work poorly (if at all). In these cases, you might have to use a little persuasion to get everything to behave. Put a strong bar (a two-by-four will do nicely) over the area you want to straighten and shim it up with thin spacers at each end. Put a padded clamp over the area of the neck that needs straightening and tighten until the neck is bent a little beyond the desired point. Tighten the trussrod and then take off the clamp to check your progress. It might take several tries to get the desired result, but you should find that if you give the trussrod a little head start the neck will straighten much more easily and with less strain on the rod. As a quick alternative to the clamp/bar arrangement, support the neck beneath the area you want to straighten, get a friend to hold down the end, and press down on the neck as you adjust the rod.

If at this point the neck still does not behave, it may be necessary to have a heat bend done, or to have some or all of the frets removed and the fingerboard planed to restore the neck to the point where the trussrod will have effect. If the neck has a pronounced upturn (ski-jump) from about the fourteenth fret to the end (precisely the area where the trussrod has little effect), extreme measures like the above will probably be required. Consult your repairperson.

Another troublesome area is that between the nut and the third or fourth fret. Here the neck is very flexible and bends more than the rest of the fingerboard when under string tension. Even though the trussrod will be effective, it is often very hard to balance straightness in this area compared to the section from the fourth fret to the twelfth. Often when you think you have the right amount of relief (when measured from the first fret to the twelfth) you find instead that it is all concentrated up around the first, second, and third frets, while the fingerboard beyond the third fret is straight. This "ramp effect" can be very pronounced in basses (it's a serious problem with guitars too), and when it occurs it plays havoc with your action adjustments because you cannot adjust it out without adversely affecting other portions of the neck.

To make things worse, most factories mill the frets with the nut already installed; the nut limits the milling file's effectiveness on the lower frets. The result is a "ramp effect" in which the lowest frets are milled less than their counterparts up the fingerboard. You may be able to remove such a ramp by carefully milling the frets by the nut. Removing the nut will make the job much easier by allowing longer file strokes over the first fret. This, however, is another job which might better be entrusted to your guitar tech, since it too could require a heat bend or fingerboard planing. Even if you can't adjust all of this ramp effect out with the trussrod, be aware of the potential problems and measure the relief from the nut to the fifth fret as well as from the fifth fret to the twelfth. You might have to leave in more relief than needed between the nut and the fifth fret in order to get the proper relief between the fifth and the twelfth frets. Try not to get a hump in the fingerboard between the fifth and the twelfth frets (measure with a 6" straightedge), because this can cause fret buzzing

problems even when you play a string open or at the first fret.

The actions on many electric basses are sensitive to changes in temperature and humidity, much more so than on most guitars. While it isn't practical to constantly readjust your bass, you should keep this thought in the back of your mind: avoid extremes in temperature whenever adjusting the action.

Adjustments at the bridge for string height and intonation shouldn't present any problems (refer to Chapter 1 for specific how-to information). Be prepared to make large changes in saddle position when adjusting for intonation. Bass strings vary greatly in manufacture (flatwound, roundwound, and polished, to name a few) and have a significant effect on the amount of compensation required. Most bridges can accommodate any kind of string, and with normal action will allow for the usual compensation adjustments. Some basses, though, have a very limited range of adjustment (Rickenbackers, for example) and are very sensitive to the type of string and action you are using when you adjust the compensation. You might have to experiment in order to find a string and action combination that will allow for accurate intonation. For a permanent solution it may be necessary to have the bridge moved to customize the instrument to your preferences.

STRING PROBLEMS

There's not much you can do when you have a bad string except to replace it. We can all tell when a string sounds bad, but how do you recognize a string that plays bad but sounds okay?

For starters, look carefully at the string when it is vibrating. If it vibrates with a nice even outline—fat in the middle and gradually tapered to a point at the ends—and dies off evenly, that's a good sign. If there appears to be motion going back and forth from end to end (a "busy" string), that's a sign of a bad string. If the string vibrations appear to get rapidly larger and smaller, that is also a sign of a bad string. Finally, look for subtle kinks in the string as well as signs of uneven diameter. Even when it is tuned to pitch, the stiffness of a string can prevent these kinks from straightening out entirely, causing yet another opportunity for fret buzzes.

Admittedly, it's hard to describe the vibration of a string, especially a bad one, because of the many variations possible. But at the very least you should stay on the lookout. A string that actually sounds bad, whether new or old, will almost certainly give you problems with fret buzzes. Don't assume that a new string is always going to be perfect. Bad strings, even when they sound okay, affect the action in a very real way because their uncontrolled vibrations add extra harmonics to the fundamental note and need more vibrating space than a string that is vibrating true. A bad string will give you fret buzz, often on random frets, misleading you into thinking that the frets and action are bad when in reality they might be in good shape.

Basses are very sensitive to string tension. Even if you replace only a single string, you will probably have to readjust the trussrod if the string is not an exact replacement. Replacing the entire set with another brand and gauge will almost certainly require a complete setup.

FINAL THOUGHTS

Be sure that there is enough down angle behind the nut as the strings go to the tuning machines. On Fender-style basses, and on other basses with a string retainer, this is normally not a problem. On other instruments the lack of downward tension behind the nut can result in loss of sustain and tone and, in extreme cases, can result in the string popping out of the nut. Most of the time the cure is simple: just wind the string onto the string post so that the windings wrap on evenly downwards toward the peghead, filling up all the space on the post. You will probably have to cut the string to do this without gaps and without overlapping.

Restringing the bass: Put enough wraps on the string post to ensure good down tension on the third and fourth strings.

If you do a lot of thumping and popping you may be able to use a slightly lower action. Striking a string percussively dampens its vibration on the initial hit, so

that it doesn't need as much space to vibrate in. Be sure your pickups are well away from the strings. Too many blows to your pickup from strings and hand will weaken its magnets and change the tone of your bass!

And finally we get to the "voodoo factor," those idiosyncrasies in the bass that create fret buzzes, bad tone, and dead spots seemingly at random, despite all of your careful setup work. While present in guitars too, these problems seem to be especially troublesome with basses.

These problems are caused by body and neck resonances present in every instrument. In acoustic instruments the body must resonate in order to get any sound at all. In electric instruments, resonances are not critical for sound production, though the degree of resonance in the body and neck will color the sound, giving the bass its particular tone. In electric basses, in addition to the resonances present in the body, the frequency range of the instrument coupled with the long necks combine to produce pronounced resonant spots on certain areas of the fingerboard. The area around the fifth to seventh frets on the G string is a well-known example, where a note played here will be instantly absorbed by the neck, producing a noticeable dead spot, as well as a weird vibration pattern in the string itself. To a lesser degree, other resonant spots also occur throughout the range of the instrument.

The point behind all this is that because of resonances built into the instrument and beyond your control, it might be impossible for you to get a completely clean action. Certainly the last thing I would want to do is leave you with the impression that since it's going to happen anyway it's okay to leave a bass with a few buzzes here and there. You should try extra hard to do the very best setup possible. If at the end there are some isolated problem areas, they won't be confused with problems that would normally be covered with basic adjustments. You then can take steps to correct or minimize them as much as possible.

An effective though expensive way to minimize resonance problems is to use a graphite neck. You can also try a different neck if yours is of the bolt-on variety. Necks vary in their degree of resonance, so this is worth trying.

Sometimes a small amount of additional neck relief will give enough clearance for an offending string to clear the frets at the trouble spot. While this involves compromises which can make the overall action stiffer, it may be the best overall solution. And finally, raising the action, as a last resort, will always be successful.

4
THE BASIC FRETMILL

Precision fretwork is always crucial for good action and tone. Together with the neck, fingerboard, and trussrod, the fretwork directly influences the adjustments that determine the amount of relief necessary for good action without buzzes. In addition, the contour and condition of the fret crown affects the tone quality, sustain, and even intonation of each note. Most likely you will have to deal with fret problems at some point during your setup work because of the great degree of precision necessary for the absolute best action and tone. It is a rare guitar, new or old, that cannot benefit from some form of leveling and contouring of the frets.

Having said this, I urge caution for anyone attempting to mill frets for the first time. It's easy enough to start hacking away at your frets; it's hard to file just the right amount at the right places without taking off any more than absolutely necessary. Needless to say, you can't put back on what you have removed, and that is really the difficulty with any sort of fret milling. Unlike most setup work, where adjustments can be returned to the original setting without harm, fretmills are unforgiving. A lot of damage can be done in just a few moments of careless filing.

If you would nevertheless like to try your hand at correcting fret problems, proceed in the following manner: First determine the problem, then decide on the steps to take to correct that problem even before removing the strings. Stick to your game plan and don't improvise.

IDENTIFYING THE PROBLEM

Several conditions call for the leveling, or milling, of frets. The most basic occurs when a fret is higher or lower than its neighbors. Because relief is necessary for the best action without fret buzzes, the neck will not be absolutely straight from one end to the other. Nevertheless, each fret has to be relatively level with respect to adjacent frets if buzzes are to be avoided. A fretmill is called for when adjusting the trussrod or tapping down a too-high fret does not work.

A second condition is a problem of poor tone caused by wear or by improper milling of the frets by the previous repairperson or by the factory. A third is the situation caused by a warped neck, an improper neck angle, or non-adjustable neck relief. While the first two conditions can normally be fixed with a basic fretmill, it is dangerous to try to alter the frets to fix a problem that is really the fault of the neck. Such repairs can be done, but they require a fair degree of skill and experience and judgment. Rather than risking generating an even bigger problem by filing the frets down to an unusable height and still not correcting the original neck condition, it would be best for you to concentrate on developing your skills on those milling jobs where the chances of complete success exist.

If after going through the complete setup procedure you find that one or more frets or fret areas are still causing buzzes, recheck your settings carefully before reaching for a file. Neck relief, string tension, and action are very closely related. Any change to one will have an immediate effect on the others, so recheck these adjustments carefully to be sure they haven't shifted. Sometimes making a change in, say, the neck relief, and readjusting the action to get the same string height will fix the problem. Or perhaps changing the string gauge and readjusting both the neck relief and the action will eliminate the buzz.

If fret buzzes persist, locate the fret or frets where they occur. Take your straightedge, hold the guitar in playing position and check for high frets. The straightedge will rock back and forth over the high ones. Sometimes a high fret will only show up on a short (6" or 3") straightedge. Often, a fret will be high beneath only one or two strings; mark the high spots with a pen.

Remember that the fret where the buzz occurs is not necessarily the culprit. You might have a buzz show up when you play on the second fret, but the high fret might actually be the eighth or ninth. This situation occurs so frequently that you should be especially careful when checking between the fifth and twelfth frets.

To eliminate any doubt as to which fret is causing the buzz, you may want to invest in a multimeter and set it up so that a string buzzing against a fret completes a circuit and shows up on the meter (see Appendix B). This will show both which fret is causing the buzz (there may be several) and what is its relative severity.

A fret grooved from string wear will let the string be pushed down further into it than a fret in good condition. The fret immediately in front of the worn one will appear to be high. Problems with worn frets can result in poor tone as well as the usual buzzes.

Worn frets: Worn frets must be leveled and recrowned. These frets show two kinds of wear. The wear from the first, second, and third strings (at top) has created narrow grooves beneath each string. The wear from the fourth, fifth, and sixth strings (at bottom) has made wider grooves from sideways finger vibrato.

Finally, check for tone. Poor tone caused by bad frets will usually take one of two forms. The first is a muffled sound with very little sustain. This is caused by a fret that is loose. Sometimes loose frets will be obvious, as when they have lifted away from the fingerboard surface, while at other times they will look and feel the same as a tight fret. Try pushing on the fret from several directions in order to observe movement, keeping in mind that, like high frets, loose frets may be loose in only a small section of their length.

The second cause of poor tone will take the form of a whining sitar-like sound. This can be caused by grooves worn into the frets from the strings, as well as frets that have been milled flat on the upper surface without being reshaped to restore their normal crowned contour. In this instance a string will buzz on the fret it is resting on (also showing that sometimes you don't need high frets to get fret buzzes). Mark frets that behave this way. Incidentally, this type of problem

tends to diminish in the upper part of the fingerboard, where the angle of the string to the fingerboard is greater.

THE FRETMILL

Now remove the strings in preparation for the mill itself. You will need:

- A 12" mill smooth file;

- A fret file or slim taper file (8");

- 320 grit and 600 grit sandpaper;

- 4/0 steel wool;

- Straightedges in 6", 12", and (optional for electric basses) 18" lengths.

You must deal with loose frets first. Try tapping them down with a small hammer so that they are level with their neighbors (be sure to support the neck directly below the loose fret with a heavy block placed on a sturdy table or workbench). Check with a short straightedge (3" or 6"), and when they are level run a drop or two of cyanoacrylate glue along the crown. Immediately wipe away any excess before it has a chance to harden on the surface of the fingerboard. If you have a fret that has pulled slightly away from the fingerboard but can easily be pushed down with your finger, you can also glue it with the cyanoacrylate by first pushing it down level with its neighbors. While holding it down apply the cyanoacrylate, wipe off the excess, and continue to hold it in position until the glue hardens. Applying an accelerator will speed up the process.

After fixing the loose frets, turn your attention to the individual high ones. Try tapping them down so that they are as level as possible with their neighbors. By tapping the frets *before* you mill them, you may be able to keep the amount of milling to an absolute minimum. Frets tapped down instead of milled will preserve more of their of their original height and will retain both sustain and tone.

If the guitar neck is not detachable from the body, cover up the pickups with masking tape. If you are working on the "kitchen table," on a guitar with a detachable neck, leave the neck attached to the body anyway. But if you have access to a workbench with a vise take the neck off whenever possible to improve access to the upper end of the fingerboard. Use a vise with padded jaws to hold the end of the neck, or screw the neck into a piece of wood that is in turn held by the vise. Without the stabilizing effect of the body, the neck will be hard to work on unless it is held securely.

Pick up the mill smooth file and prepare for the actual milling of the frets. First, take a close look at the file. Check it end-for-end against a straightedge to make sure that it is tapered slightly in thickness over the upper third of its length. It should rock slightly. These files are rarely perfectly flat to the same degree on both sides. The straightedge should rock slightly more on one surface than on the other. Mark your file so that you can keep track of the straightness on each side. As we will see, this characteristic can be used to your advantage.

If the nut can be removed easily you should take it out, as this will make it much easier to file the frets level in the area near the nut. Most nuts can be removed by first scoring the finish around them and then carefully tapping them loose with a woodblock held against the surface facing the fingerboard. Fender-style nuts, set in a slot in the fingerboard, should be scored and tapped on both sides. The nut must be carefully lifted straight up (use a pair of pliers or an end-nipper). If there is a lot of finish built up, removing the nut might be more bother than it's worth, but remember to file carefully so that you don't build up a "ramp" on the first two or three frets.

Support the neck in the area where you plan to file, and use the side of the file where the ends curve up slightly. This will allow best control of the file for most of the milling procedure. Take slow passes at first along the length of the neck and check the frets after each pass to see which ones are being hit. You will see a shiny line on top of each fret where the file has re-moved material. For a basic mill, your goal is to file evenly so that there is a shiny line on every fret, indi-cating that all the frets are level with their neighbors. Use a felt-tip marking pen to darken the fret tops if you have trouble seeing where you have filed. You may have to re-mark the fret tops several times during the course of a mill. If you have grooves worn into the fret from string wear, file the frets so that the grooves are removed. If you have a few frets with very deep grooves, complete removal of the grooves might not be practical because the surrounding frets might have to

be milled so low that the overall fret height will be too low for proper sustain and tone. You can raise these frets slightly (for experts only!) or you can leave them alone. For the most part, a few minor grooves in the frets will not hurt the overall action very much anyway, though string bends will not be as smooth as they could be. In any event, a conservative approach to fret milling is generally best.

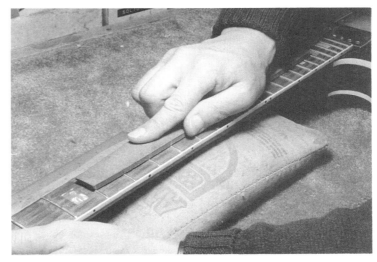

Milling the frets: Support the neck when milling the frets. Initially, take long lengthwise passes with the file.

Checking your progress: After the frets have been milled there will be a shiny flat area across the top of each fret, indicating that it is level with its neighbors.

When filing the frets near the nut, make short strokes so that the file is continuously in contact with each fret. If you have to take a lot of material off the first few frets, turn the file over to the flatter side so that more of its tip comes into contact with the first fret, and move your neck support below the first fret.

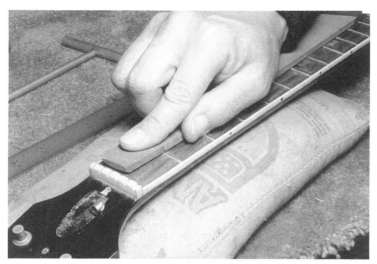

Milling in critical areas: When working on critical areas use short strokes. Support the neck from below and hold the file directly above the frets being worked on.

Check frequently with your straightedge. Your goal should be a straight neck between the first and twelfth frets. If you feel you have the control, try to build in a little relief on the bass side. Don't overdo it—two or three thousandths should be enough. You want to avoid at all costs having relief on the treble side and none (or a hump in the middle) on the bass side. If your neck is like this, you can try to correct it by filing the frets in the middle area of the neck on the bass side, and at the ends of the neck (around the first and around the twelfth) on the treble side. Again, be conservative in your filing and don't try to get fancy if you aren't absolutely sure that you can correct a problem without filing the frets away to nothing.

Whenever checking the neck for straightness, hold the guitar in playing position. You may have to occasionally readjust the neck slightly as you mill the frets if you find that the file is not hitting the right frets. For example, if you are having trouble filing the first few frets evenly, loosening the trussrod will relax the neck and put more of the end of the fingerboard in contact with the file. If you need to take out a hump in the neck between the fifth and twelfth frets, it may help to tighten the trussrod in order to accent the hump and expose more of these frets to the file.

If your guitar doesn't have a trussrod you should remember that its neck will always pull up under string tension. Keeping in mind the original relief in the neck under tension (you did remember to measure the relief before you removed the strings, didn't you?) file the frets so that the same relief is maintained. If there was too much relief, try filing a little more on the first few frets, and if there wasn't enough relief, file a little more

in the middle of the fingerboard. Without an adjustable trussrod, the neck will probably be bowed back without the string tension, making it something of a guessing game as to how much to file and where.

Experienced guitar repairpeople develop an intuitive feel for how much to file and where as well as tricks to simulate string tension, ranging from adjustment of the neck supports to pushing or pulling on the neck in various areas while the milling is going on, to jigs as used by Dan Erlewine.(*Guitar Player Repair Guide* by Dan Erlewine, GPI Books) If you don't understand what is going on, take the safe approach and file evenly. Remember, the goal of the basic fretmill is to get rid of high spots rather than to correct deficiencies in neck relief and construction.

RESTORING THE CROWN

After you have leveled the frets, you will have to re-shape them in order to restore their original crowned contour. As I mentioned earlier, one of the reasons for working on frets is to correct tone problems caused by poorly milled or seriously worn frets. Proper contouring and polishing of the fret crown is vitally important for clear tone and long sustain. It may take you as long or longer to do this part of the fretmill than the leveling, but attention to this detail will help to ensure that your guitar will sound its best.

You have a choice of two methods to do the contouring of the frets. The simplest and best choice for most people is to use a fret file specially made for the purpose. They come in several sizes, depending upon the width of the fret, and do a good job of reshaping the crown. File along the length of the fret, taking care to observe its shape as you file. Be absolutely sure that you do not take off any material from its top. You may have to angle the file slightly in order to get into the edge of the fret next to the fingerboard, but this shouldn't be a problem unless the fret has already been milled low. Be careful not to nick the fingerboard, though—you may want to cover it next to the frets with a layer of masking tape for a little insurance.

Another method is to use a slim taper file—otherwise known as a three-corner file—available from any hardware store. It should be about eight inches long and very sharp. Angle it against the side of the fret as you file along the fret's length. By varying the angle as you file you can duplicate the curved original contour. You must brace the file against the fingers of your free hand as you file as it is very easy to slip if care is not taken. As with the fret file, you may want to tape up the fingerboard. I do all of my fret contouring with the slim taper file because it is easier to get into the edge of the fret next to the fingerboard (especially with very low frets) and is adaptable to any size of fretwire. It is also faster (though this is of no concern to anyone except a professional), but undeniably riskier for the beginner. You can put some pretty deep nicks in the fingerboard if you aren't careful.

Recrowning the frets: After leveling the frets, recrown them using a slim taper file (pictured) or a fret file. This photo and the next show how to hold the file, using the thumb as a guide.

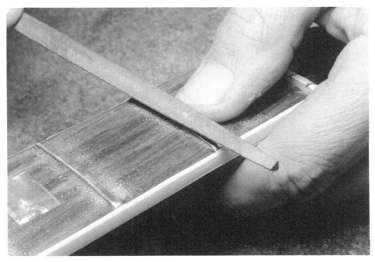

Recrown both sides of the fret. Use masking tape to protect the finish when working on lacquered fingerboards.

With either method, file until only a thin line of the original flat milled surface remains on the top of the fret. At this point you can switch to 320 grit sandpaper folded two or three times and sand lengthwise along the fingerboard. If your fingerboard is rosewood or ebony, there is no need to cover it. If you have a maple or finished fingerboard, cover it with masking tape

before sanding. Sand just until all the file marks are removed and then switch to 600 grit sandpaper. Sand until the marks left by the 320 grit paper have been removed. In order to get into the corners between frets and fingerboard, try using a rectangular pencil eraser reshaped into a half-round edge. Wrap the sandpaper around it and sand slowly in a lengthwise direction, so that the sandpaper will get into the corners as much as possible. Sand only as much as is necessary to eliminate the marks left by the previous operation. Excess sanding can destroy the levelness of the frets. Finish with 4/0 steel wool in both lengthwise and crosswise directions. You should end up with nicely rounded and polished crowns on each fret. Clean up the fingerboard with a soft cloth (you can use a little lemon oil if you want, to seal and to bring out the wood grain), and take special care to completely remove all of the steel wool dust.

Smoothing the frets: Sand lengthwise along the fingerboard until the marks from the previous filing or sanding are gone.

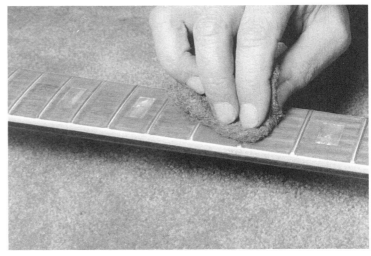

Polishing the frets: Polish the frets and fingerboard with 4/0 steel wool.

Final Touches

Reassemble the neck to the body—or, if the body and neck are in one piece, remove the masking tape from the pickups—and restring the instrument. Reinstall the nut if necessary, go through the basic setup adjustments, and check the frets for buzzes and tone. You should notice an improvement in both. If you have taken care, you should usually get satisfactory results the first time. In some cases—it happens to the pros, too—one or two frets might have to be touched up. Don't be discouraged if this happens, because the reaction of the neck and trussrod to the tension of the strings is not completely predictable. If you decide to do the frets again, concentrate only on the fret or frets that are causing problems. Mark the affected frets with a felt-tip pen so you will know exactly where you are filing. Chances are that only a minimal amount of filing and polishing will be required the second time around.

Incidentally, you might get a fret buzz from a string that is vibrating on the fingerboard behind the fretted position. This is caused by a sympathetic vibration of the string in response to the fretted note (usually an octave interval) and is generally more noticeable on the lower strings. At certain combinations of neck relief and nut height the string behind the fretted note will begin to vibrate in sympathy, and if it is close to one or more frets it will buzz on those frets. Usually, raising or lowering the nut slightly will cure the noise with little effect on the action.

Beyond the scope of this book are those areas of fretwork that go beyond basic adjustments and take on aspects of actual repairs. For example, some neck warp and neck relief problems can be corrected with fretmills. Some cases of "ski jump" at the end of the neck can also be helped with fretmills. And fretting-out problems can also be minimized by selective milling. Finally, there are judgment calls where, in the long run, reworking the fingerboard and refretting would be preferable to keeping things working temporarily with a mill. These advanced fretmill concepts and examples are really repair topics and, like the process of refretting an instrument, are best covered separately.

While I have taken quite a bit of space to explain the basics of milling frets, all of this detail is necessary so that you can proceed with a clearly defined goal and avoid the pitfalls that can plague novices (and professionals). You might ask, is this all I need to know about fretmills? Definitely not. But within the province of setup and action adjustments, the fundamentals described here will allow you to do a successful fretmill, get the action down without fret buzzes, and enjoy the satisfaction of having done it yourself.

5
PLAYING IN TUNE

It's a fact—some trips to the repairshop to fix intonation problems are unnecessary. It's also a fact that some guitar players don't know how to tune a guitar, no matter how long they have been playing. Should we conclude, then, that these players are idiots? Or is it that they don't fully understand the tuning methods that ensure accurate intonation? I'm just kidding about the idiot part, of course, but there is a lot of misunderstanding about guitar tuning that prevents players from tuning their instruments accurately.

Equal temperament

The most important point to remember is that guitar tuning is based on the concept of the equal-tempered scale (for a more complete discussion of equal-tempered tuning, see *Complete Guitar Repair* by Hideo Kamimoto, Oak Publications). In the equal-tempered scale, the ratio of one note to the next is 1.0594631 (the 12th root of 2) to 1, and there are twelve equally spaced semitones in an octave. Theoretically we would like all intervals between notes to sound pure, or without beats. In practice, though, only unison and octave intervals can be pure. All other intervals, such as those between the open strings of the guitar, have to be altered slightly (equalized) in order to have all chords in all keys play equally in tune. For example, the perfect fourth interval between the sixth-string E and the fifth-string A must be tuned slightly wider than pure by a very small amount (about two cents, or two hundredths of a semitone). The major third between the third-string G and the second-string B must be widened by about fourteen cents, a noticeable amount. In like fashion, all other intervals except the octave must be adjusted slightly wide or narrow. This translates into the occurrence of beats whenever two notes are played together. The rhythmic throbbing as two notes of slightly differing frequency reinforce and subtract from each other is hardly noticeable on some intervals, like fourths or fifths, but is prominent in minor and major thirds.

Instruments tuned in equal temperament, such as guitars and pianos, cannot be adjusted to play in theoretically perfect tune, where all intervals around the fingerboard will be pure. They can, however, be adjusted to sound very acceptably in tune in all keys, provided the player tunes correctly and the maker or repairperson sets up the intonation within the guidelines of equal temperament.

Some popular tuning methods

What is the best way to tune your guitar? I'll have suggestions a little later on, but before getting into details, let's survey some popular tuning methods to see what advantages and shortcomings each of them has. You may find your own tuning method described here, and if you are having tuning problems the suggestions that follow might prove useful.

Open-string tuning: This method, in which you listen to the intervals between adjacent pairs of strings ("tuning by ear") is the simplest way since none of the strings are fretted. It is difficult unless you have developed plenty of practice in detecting the way equalized fourth intervals (E to A, A to D, D to G, B to E) and third intervals (G to B) should sound. With practice you can quickly get your instrument up to pitch this way when every string needs tuning, such as when restringing. Even when you can do it accurately, though, this isn't necessarily the best way to tune because none of the strings are fretted. If you haven't intonated your guitar, or if you have old strings, it won't play in tune when fretted. On the other hand, if it has previously been set up properly with fresh strings this is an excellent way to quickly make minor adjustments.

The four-five method: This is probably the most popular method, because you only have to match the pitch between adjacent strings. The best way to tune with this method is to first tune one string to a standard pitch such an A tuning fork (440hz). You can do this by fretting and playing the first string at the fifth fret and matching its pitch to the tuning fork. Then match the second-string, fifth-fret E to the open first string. Then tune the third-string, fourth-fret B to the open second string. Match the fourth-string, fifth-fret G, then the fifth-string D, then the sixth-string A, all to their higher neighbors. When you are finished the open sixth-string

E should be exactly two octaves below the open first string.

Here is a tip for speeding things up. To tune the second (B) string, play the open first-string E by brushing across it with the index finger of the right hand—at the fifth fret. Immediately hammer on to the second string with the same finger at the fifth fret. You now have both strings ringing and the second string fretted, leaving your left hand free to simultaneously tune the second string while listening to both strings at the same time. Use the same technique in turn for the third, fourth, fifth, and sixth strings.

If your guitar's intonation has been accurately set, the four-five method can be effective because it takes into account the required compensation, the gauge and tension of the string, and the accuracy of the finger-board. However, getting precisely in tune this way is difficult because errors can accumulate as you move down the strings. An intonation error on one string will throw off the strings following it. Nevertheless, the four-five is basically a good method, especially when you continue and crosscheck it with others. Because small errors in tuning become more pronounced the higher up you play, the four-five method is best suited for tuning when most of the playing will be in the lower part of the fingerboard.

The harmonics method: Another tuning method uses harmonics. Match the first string at the fifth fret to A440 from a tuning fork. Then tune the sixth-string E either by listening to the two-octave interval between it and the open first string or by playing it while a left-hand finger barely touches it at the fifth fret to produce an E harmonic in unison with the first string. Tune so you can't hear any beating.

Next match the E harmonic on the fifth string, seventh fret with the E harmonic on the sixth string, fifth fret. Repeat between the fourth and fifth, and the third and fourth strings. Then skip to the second and first strings. Play the harmonics in the same way, but tune the second string. The fourth-fret harmonic on the third string can be compared to the fifth-fret harmonic on the second string.

You should remember that harmonics are pure intervals, and other than at the octave interval they cannot be relied upon for accurate intonation because of the limitations of equal temperament. While most of the strings can be tuned fairly accurately with harmonics (these are fifth-interval harmonics, and the difference

between the pure harmonic intervals and the equal-tempered fret intervals is small), the third-string to second-string interval will be badly off. This is because the third-string, fourth-fret B harmonic—a pure major third above the open G—is substantially different from the equal-tempered third. No matter how much you try, you can't tune these harmonics to be pure (without beats) and still get the high and low E strings to play in octaves.

Tuning by harmonics is convenient for an initial rough tuning because the notes will ring without your fretting the strings. But because all of the pitches are open, the method is subject to the same limitations as open-string tuning. Use it selectively and only in conjunction with other tuning methods.

Chords: Everyone plays chords to test their tuning, and this is really the final test for any method. Make sure that all chords sound good on all strings and over the entire fingerboard. But by now, since you know the basic principles of equal-tempered tuning and the impossibility of tuning to pure intervals, you should be aware of the potential pitfalls when listening to chords. For example, retuning your guitar so that a chord "sounds good," especially after having tuned with one or more methods, completely subverts the goal of getting the guitar equally well in tune all over the fingerboard and in all keys. When you tune your guitar so that a single chord sounds perfectly in tune you are tuning for pure intervals, and while that one chord may sound perfect, others will sound very much out of tune. Use chords only to check the accuracy of your tuning by other methods. If you find errors, go back to your original methods and retune.

The octave method: Since we know that only the octave and unison are pure intervals and that checking for such variables as intonation at the bridge, string height at the nut, overall action, strings that are true, and even pickup interaction, require actual fretting of the string, my recommendation for tuning is that you incorporate octave intervals during your final tuning. By comparing octaves across the strings and on different parts of the fingerboard, you can tune your guitar precisely and emphasize intonation accuracy on selected parts of the neck.

Here is a basic octave tuning routine that favors the middle of the fingerboard and eliminates the effect of cumulative tuning errors. First set the pitch of the first string E using a tuning fork or other pitch standard. Next tune the sixth-string E exactly two octaves below that—you can use the open low E, the harmonic E on the fifth fret, or the fretted E on the twelfth fret. Then match the second-string, fifth-fret E to the open E of the first string. Match the third-string, ninth-fret E to the open first string. Tune the fourth-string, second- (or fourteenth-) fret E to the first string. Finally, tune the fifth-string, seventh-fret E an octave below the open first string.

Do an additional octave check by fretting various string pairs. Since errors in tuning become more critical in the upper fret positions, do this check in the area between the seventh and twelfth frets. Compare each string with several others to check octave intervals thoroughly over every part of the fingerboard. If during these crosschecks a string shows up as consistently flat or sharp, recheck your setup and adjust as required.

In the real world, a combination of tuning methods is usually used. For quick, rough tuning, open-string tuning or harmonics work well. For the next stage, use the four-five comparison method. This method can also be used for the quick initial stage if the notes are both fretted and played with one hand. If you take care, this might be all you need. Where tuning is critical, finish up with the octave method, comparing octaves in the area of the fingerboard where you do most of your playing. And keep in mind that whenever you fret a string you should use the same finger pressure as you would when actually playing. Unusually light or heavy finger pressure will alter the pitch of the string as will sideways pressure.

Stretch tuning

There is another facet of tuning that adds an additional layer of complexity to your usual tuning process because it is psychological and does not lend itself well to scientific measurement. This is the principle of stretch tuning.

For many musicians, guitar players included, what the ear "wants to hear" is slightly different from what would be considered accurate tuning as measured by either tuning devices or by interval comparisons, either pure or tempered. Professional piano tuners are very accustomed to tuning slightly sharper as they move up the octaves. Your brain, when comparing intervals, interprets this slight sharpness in the upper note as being more pleasing, brighter, livelier, and more "in tune" than an interval that is exactly in tune when measured by beats or by an electronic tuner.

(Interestingly, at least one guitar company acknowledged the benefits of stretch tuning. Gretsch guitars in the mid-sixties featured on some models a "T-Zone Tempered Treble" fingerboard. Frets above the twelfth were slanted slightly so that the treble strings would play slightly sharper than the bass strings. The idea had merit but lacked refinement and the feature never caught on.)

Of course, since the piano has seven-plus octaves versus the guitar's four or fewer, the stretching of the octaves need be far less pronounced on a guitar. It takes only a few cents sharpening on the high E to make a noticeable difference in how your ear perceives the sound. This may seem at odds with everything previously mentioned on how to adjust your intonation and how to tune your guitar, but the bottom line is to end up with an instrument that sounds pleasing to the ear—regardless of the measurements on the tuner.

If you have access to a good guitar tuner (one that can accurately distinguish increments of a cent) and if you have a guitar with adjustable saddles, you can easily test stretch tuning for yourself. Tune your open first-string E using your tuner. Now play the octave E at the twelfth fret and compare it with the open E. Adjust the first-string bridge saddle so that, by ear, the twelfth-fret E sounds exactly an octave higher than the open E. Play alternately the open E and the twelfth-fret E (don't use the harmonic) and adjust the bridge saddle forward and backward until the octave interval sounds best to your ear.

Now check the tuning of the open E with the twelfth-fret E with your tuner and see if the octave interval that you tuned by ear is the same as the octave interval measured by your tuner. Chances are that the high E as measured by your ear will be slightly sharper than the open E. If this turns out to be the case, you should probably incorporate stretch tuning whenever you adjust the intonation on your guitar. All you have to do is use slightly less compensation at the bridge so that each note will play progressively sharper the higher up the fingerboard you go. This only has to be done on the first and second strings (be sure that the other strings never play flat). It takes only a few cents sharpness at the twelfth fret to make a noticeable difference. Keep in mind that because this is a subjective judgment, the adjustment must be done by ear. Although I recommend stretch tuning whenever intonating a guitar (when it is practical to do so), it is up to you to decide whether or not the method results in a tuning that pleases you. It's worth a try, and the outcome may give your intonation adjustments that final touch of perfection.

Guitar Tuners

Instead of using various "manual" methods to tune your guitar, you may choose to use an electronic tuner as an aid. Since with a tuner you do all pitch comparisons visually—whether it be by means of an indicating needle, strobe disc, or light indicator—you don't even have to listen to your instrument as you tune it. Under certain circumstances this might be an advantage, such as when you have to tune under noisy conditions.

Strobe tuners: The original tuners used strobe discs illuminated by flashing neon lights, the frequency of flashes determined by the pitch of the signal being fed in. In fact, the term "strobe tuning," meaning adjusting the intonation of a guitar with the aid of a tuner, came about when stroboscope-type tuners were the only tuners available. The earliest such device intended for musical instruments was called the Stroboconn and used twelve geared strobe discs so that several notes (chords, for example) could be tested simultaneously. A simpler version, the Strobotuner, had only one disc with a selector switch to set it up for each note. Current equivalents are made by Peterson and are accurate but expensive.

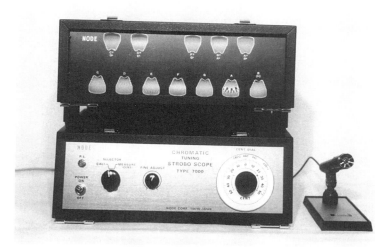

Peterson strobe tuners: Strobe tuners such as the Peterson single-note and chromatic models are very accurate and register the note instantly.

Expense aside, strobe tuners react instantly to pitch changes, and the multi-wheel versions can test any note or combination of notes without your having to change any switch settings. Strobe tuners are the only guitar tuners that can easily measure changes in pitch down to one cent, making them the preferred tuners for precise testing and measuring in the repairshop. They are also not affected very much by non-musical noise.

Quartz tuners: Most other tuners are portable quartz-controlled solid-state units in which a needle or light indicates correct pitch. They usually allow you to plug an electric guitar into them in line with the cord to the amp. Most also have a built-in microphone for picking up acoustic instruments. While most of these quartz tuners work adequately, their performance varies widely and not necessarily according to price. Features such as readability, reaction time, accuracy, and sensitivity should all be considered. Electric bass players should be especially careful because some tuners work poorly at low frequencies. Some require selector switches for each note, while others automatically indicate the desired note but are limited to the open strings of the guitar. Still others are fully chromatic and automatic. All are reasonably priced (moderately expensive to dirt cheap) and represent excellent value considering the complexity of the technology.

Quartz tuners

Be especially critical when testing for stability and reaction time. All of these tuners will give a steady reading for only a short time before becoming unstable and dying. Tuners that exhibit steady readings give you more time to read the output and make accurate comparisons. Keep in mind that they also take a fraction of a second to give you a reading. This can be frustrating when you are trying to tune quickly. If you are interested in using your tuner for more than just casual tuning, such as for making or adjusting compensated saddles or for checking fret placement, get one that will indicate the full chromatic scale as well as operate automatically.

While the easiest way to use a guitar tuner is to just play each string and adjust the tuning of each open string, accuracy will be limited by the same factors that affect aural tuning methods. You will be able to get the guitar in tune quickly, but for the final precision tuning use octaves and unisons on the upper part of the fingerboard (as described above) and listen carefully while watching the meter readings. Regardless of what the manufacturers say about the accuracy of their tuners, your ear can do a better job of distinguishing small errors when comparing octave and unison intervals.

FINE-TUNING YOUR GUITAR'S INTONATION

If you have set up your guitar and adjusted everything within the parameters of equal-temperament, and if you have tuned your guitar carefully using the suggestions outlined above, it should play quite well over the entire fingerboard. For most people this is all that is necessary; in fact, even getting this far is a satisfying accomplishment. Considering all the variables that exist, not to mention the changes that can occur daily—changes in the guitar's structure due to temperature and humidity, and false strings due to manufacturing errors as well as normal wear—just maintaining consistent intonation over a period of time requires a fair investment of time and energy.

Persistent intonation problems

On the other hand some of you may get to this point and still not be happy with the way your instrument tunes. Both your guitar tuner and your ears may indicate that everything is in tune, and yet you might be experiencing the feeling that somehow, it still doesn't sound quite right. If you have truly exhausted all the possibilities in your attempts to set up your guitar, adjust the intonation and do a final tuning. The following comments might be of interest.

Beats: First, hearing beats when you compare equal-tempered chord intervals might be especially disturbing to you if you have sensitive (and well-trained) ears. As I mentioned before, equal temperament allows for equally good intonation in all keys and on all intervals. With fretted instruments, though, there is not much you can do to improve on this situation if you don't want to be limited only to certain keys and chords. Piano players have the same problem, and while they might not be entirely happy with equal-tempered tuning either, other tuning and keyboard arrangements have not proven to be practical in the long run. So you will have to adjust to the instrument and come to terms with the compromises required by equal temperament. Frankly, problems of this type are rare, and in most musical situations the non-pure intervals of equal-tempered tuning are not noticeable. If you are still not happy, I would advise that you recheck all of your adjustments and seek the advice of a competent repairperson or an experienced guitar player.

Lower fingerboard area: If you have problems with the strings playing sharp at the first or second frets, remember that the string height at the nut should be set a few thousandths higher than absolutely necessary in order to allow for harder playing on the open strings. This extra string height at the nut will introduce a small amount of additional pitch sharpness when the strings are fretted on the first few frets. With certain string, action, and fretwire combinations (typically high actions, tall fretwire, and light-gauge strings) this may be especially noticeable.

Beyond experimenting with your guitar's action, string gauges, and your fingering pressure, you might try compensating the nut. This requires that you move it forward toward the bridge a bit. As at the saddle, each string will require a different amount of compensation. Another possibility (beyond the scope of this book) is a compensated fingerboard! You should consult a competent repairperson and have your intonation checked out on an accurate strobe tuner before having this type of work done.

Upper fingerboard area: Intonation is often slightly off at the extreme upper end of the fingerboard, even when compensation is perfect at the twelfth fret. Because most guitarists do not play much at this end of the fingerboard, this is normally not a big problem. On the other hand, those who are really critical about their tuning should be aware of the situation and how to correct the problem if it becomes serious.

Intonation can go both sharp and flat at the upper end of the fingerboard. A slight upturn or downturn beyond the twelfth fret will have a noticeable effect on the intonation because the effect will be the same as changing string height above the fingerboard. In addition, strings that are not absolutely true or are worn will make more problems in the upper ranges. Most of the time the strings will play flat. This is because string compensation, which is normally done at the twelfth fret, gets progressively larger in proportion to the remaining string length on each successive fret beyond the twelfth. For example, a compensation of 1/16" on a 25" scale is a quarter of a percent of the total string length. That same 1/16" compensation is still there when you play above the twelfth fret, but now the effective scale length is 12-1/2", and the compensation has doubled to half a percent of the total.

So why don't we just set the compensation on a fret above the twelfth fret? This could be done with an accurate strobe tuner; if the guitar has twenty-four frets, an octave comparison could be made by comparing the second-octave harmonic at the twenty-fourth fret with the fretted second-octave note. Would the results give improved intonation over the whole fingerboard? It depends. In practical terms, simply intonating and compensating the bridge at a higher fret position may improve intonation in the area where the guitar was intonated, but chances are that the intonation will be worse in the lower areas of the fingerboard where most of the actual playing is done. This is due in part to variations in fingerboard straightness (including relief) and string trueness, which are not constant from one end of the fingerboard to the other. In addition, if the nut is not compensated and the open strings are high enough at the nut to cause intonation problems on the lower portion of the fingerboard, intonating at the extreme upper end will make intonation problems at the lower end even worse. Take note of the fact that if you compensate at the nut the guitar will require less compensation at the bridge. This adjustment alone may improve intonation over the entire fingerboard.

This discussion of the more obscure points of intonation isn't for everyone. But while these concerns may not apply to most guitars and players, it would be a serious omission to not mention them at all. Sooner or later you will find yourself in a situation where standard intonation and tuning procedures will not work. It may be with a non-standard tuning, or with some unusual combination of strings and action. It may be as straightforward as trying to get a twelve-string guitar to *really* play in tune! In any event, the solution will probably be beyond the scope of basic adjustments. Take your guitar to your favorite repairpeople and see what they think.

6
GUITAR HARDWARE SHOWCASE

The main adjustment areas for electric guitars—the nut, trussrod, and bridge—vary considerably from guitar to guitar. Given the variety of styles and the difficulty of describing adjustment procedures with text alone, I have provided in this chapter some photos that I hope will acquaint you with the wide range of hardware used on electrics both old and new.

Many features shown here have been selected to illustrate well-known designs common to many popular guitars. I have also sought to highlight some not-so-common features and instruments. In addition to providing adjustment instructions, I have listed the tools you would need. By using this chapter together with the instructions given in earlier parts of the book you should be able to successfully set up just about any instrument.

TREMOLO BRIDGES

G&L SC-2

Tools required: Bridge height: 1/8" allen
Saddle height: .050" allen
Intonation: phillips screwdriver

The G & L SC-2 tremolo bridge with knife-edge pivots.

Paul Reed Smith

Tools required: Intonation: phillips screwdriver
Saddle height: .050" allen

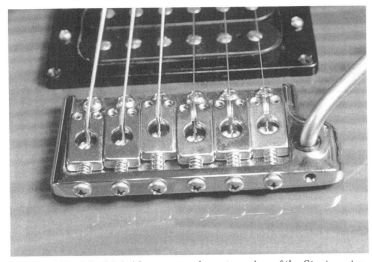

The Paul Reed Smith bridge, a very elegant version of the Stratocaster tremolo bridge. Adjustable tension for the tremolo arm.

Epiphone with Steinberger bridge

Tools required: Saddle height and lock: 1.5mm allen

The Steinberger bridge (installed on a Strat-style Epiphone) is an all-adjustable bridge with several unique features. An allen wrench on the left side of the base locks all of the saddles at one time. The thumbscrews lock the individual strings, and a lever (just behind the word "LOCK") disables the tremolo. The bent lever at the rear adjusts trem spring tension.

Fender Stratocaster (Custom Shop)

Tools required: Bridge pivot and intonation: phillips screwdriver
Saddle height: .050" allen

The traditional-style Stratocaster tremolo bridge on a Fender Custom Shop Strat. This bridge features stamped sheet-metal saddles and six bridge pivot screws. This classic design is fully adjustable and is the basis for many similar designs, both by Fender and by others.

Fender Jaguar

Tools required: Saddle height, bridge height: .050" allen
Intonation: phillips screwdriver

The Fender Jaguar bridge. The adjustments for intonation and saddle height are easily seen. The overall bridge height adjustment is with an allen wrench inserted through the small holes at either end of the bridge. Because of the tremolo tailpiece, the bridge "rocks" on thimbles set in the body: be sure the bridge is set vertically when adjusting intonation.

Fender Jazzmaster

Tools required: Bridge height, saddle height: .050" allen
Saddle height: phillips screwdriver

The Fender Jazzmaster bridge is similar to that of the Jaguar but lacks the mute.

Mosrite 6-string

Tools required: Intonation: phillips screwdriver
Bridge height: flat-blade screwdriver

The Mosrite adjustable bridge. Overall bridge height and intonation are adjustable, but the roller saddles (the guitar has a vibrato tailpiece) prevent individual string-height adjustment. The saddles can rattle and cause loss of sustain if they do not fit tightly to the base.

Non-Tremolo Bridges

Gibson Les Paul '59 Reissue

Tools required: Intonation: small flat-blade screwdriver

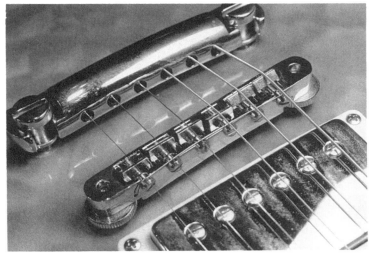

The famous Gibson Tune-O-Matic bridge installed on a '59 LP Reissue. With only detail changes (the original model didn't have the wire saddle retainer), this is the bridge that made it possible to adjust Gibsons precisely for each individual string—and inspired countless copies along the way. Currently only metal saddles are used, though for many years nylon saddles were offered as well. Gibson has used these bridges on just about all of their electric guitars. When Bigsby or other vibrato tailpieces are used, a tapered thumbwheel is installed so that the bridge can "rock" in response to string movement. While these bridges are usually installed with the saddle adjusting screw heads pointing toward the pickup, they must be installed with the screw heads facing the tailpiece whenever a vibrato tailpiece is used so that the screw heads will not work themselves up and touch the strings. The saddles are easily reversed when it is necessary to obtain more travel for intonation adjustments. Individual string height is adjusted by the depth of the notch.

Fender Telecaster USA

Tools required: Saddle height: .050" allen
Intonation: phillips screwdriver

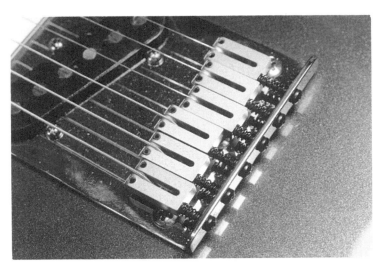

A six-way adjustable bridge on a Fender American Standard Telecaster. Several different styles of six-way adjustable bridges are used on the Telecaster.

Fender Telecaster Mexican Standard

Tools required: Saddle height: 1.5mm allen
Intonation: phillips screwdriver

A six-way bridge, as used on the Fender Mexican Standard Telecaster. Not as modern in appearance as the one used on the American Standard Tele, but just as functional.

Fender Custom Esquire

Tools required: Saddle height: small flat-blade screwdriver
Intonation: phillips screwdriver

The traditional Tele/Esquire bridge. This three-way adjustable model is simple in style but does not intonate as accurately (in stock form) as a six-way bridge. A simple modification (see section on setting up Telecasters) will allow for accurate intonation on all strings. The flange on the bridge base allows for a bridge cover, which is rarely used.

Gibson Les Paul Standard

Tools required: Intonation: small flat-blade screwdriver

The Nashville Tune-O-Matic bridge, installed on a Gibson Les Paul Standard. This bridge, used on many Gibson models, is an improved version of the original, with additional saddle travel, stronger bridge height adjusters, and rattle-free operation.

Gibson Firebrand 335S

Tools required: Saddle adjustments: small flat-blade screwdriver

Another Nashville Tune-O-Matic, this time installed on a Firebrand 335S. The fine-tuning stop tailpiece is available as a replacement for the standard stop tailpiece.

Gibson L6-S

Tools required: Bridge height: flat-blade screwdriver
Intonation: small flat-blade screwdriver

The L6-S sports a Schaller "Harmonica" bridge. Extra-long saddle travel can accommodate any string/action combination. The saddles can be adjusted from both sides of the bridge.

Gretsch Chet Atkins

The Gretsch roller bridge. The rollers give adjustable string spacing and move with the strings when the tremolo is used. The adjustable bridge base allows for height adjustment, but intonation adjustment is poor because string length for each saddle cannot be adjusted individually.

Ibanez Standard

Tools required: All adjustments: flat-blade screwdriver

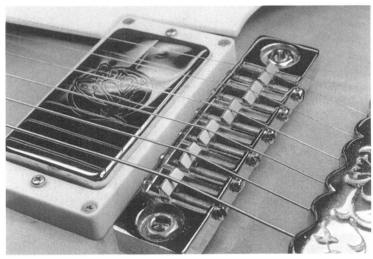

The Ibanez version of the Schaller harmonica bridge. This bridge features extra-long saddle travel plus a locknut on the height adjustment screw to hold the bridge tightly without rocking.

Gretsch Country Club

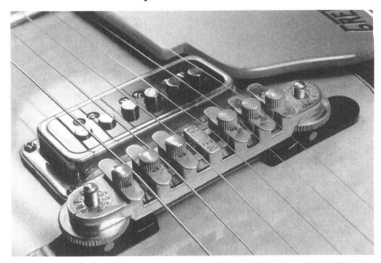

The famous Melita bridge installed on a Gretsch Country Club. This is Gretsch's version of the Tune-O-Matic bridge. Adjustments can be done without tools but the bulky construction makes it a little hard to "palm" the bridge.

Gretsch Melita bridge

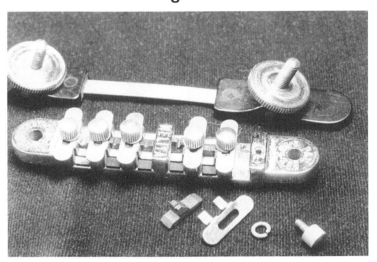

The Gretsch Melita bridge. All of the features of the Gibson Tune-O-Matic—with twice the parts.

Peavey T-15

Tools required: Bridge height: 1/8" allen
Saddle intonation: 1/16" allen

The Peavey T-15 guitar features basic bridge adjustments only. Note the saddle offset, which is designed for use with a plain third string. This is a sensible feature for a rock-and-roll guitar.

Rickenbacker

The Rickenbacker six-string bridge. All features are similar to the bridge on the model 360 twelve-string guitar except for the single notch on each saddle. The bridge sits on indentations in the base plate; the base plate can be moved if intonation is out of range.

Fine-Tuning Tailpiece

Gibson Firebird

Tools required: Bridge height: flat-blade screwdriver
Intonation: small flat-blade screwdriver

A Schaller bridge/fine tuning tailpiece combination on a Gibson Firebird. This bridge is a conversion for the original stop-tailpiece bridge. (See also Gibson Firebrand 335S.)

Tailpiece-Bridges

Gibson ES-225

The stop-tailpiece bridge, trapeze style, used on a Gibson ES-225. Similar in design and features to the one used on the Les Paul gold top, but is made in an "over" style. It has the same shortcomings, but you can "palm" this one.

Gibson Melody Maker

Tools required: Intonation: 3/32" allen
Height: flat-blade screwdriver

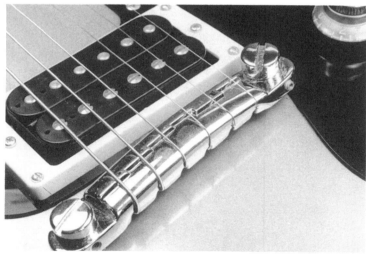

A Gibson Melody Maker with stop-tailpiece bridge—this time with a compensated "saddle" cast into the bridge. While it is adjustable for height and overall compensation, this compensation—typical of earlier electric guitars—is not suited for rock-and-roll strings. For an example of correct compensation on a fixed saddle, see the Peavey T-15.

Gibson Les Paul Junior, 1957

Tools required: Intonation: 3/32" allen
Height: flat-blade screwdriver

The Gibson Les Paul Junior, circa 1957, with stop-tailpiece bridge. This bridge has a very limited range for intonation adjustment. The Badass bridge conversion, with individually adjustable saddles, was specifically designed to replace it.

Gibson Les Paul gold top

Tools required: Intonation: nutdriver or small socket wrench

A trapeze-style stop-tailpiece bridge on an early Les Paul gold top. The nuts on each end of the bridge offer limited intonation adjustment. This is an "under" version, with the strings wrapping underneath the bar. Other variations of this bridge have the strings going over the bar. Adjustment for action is via the thumbscrews at each end of the bridge.

TWELVE-STRING ELECTRICS

Rickenbacker 360-12

Tools required: Intonation: 5/64" allen
Bridge height: 3/32" allen

Rickenbacker 360 twelve-string guitars use a six-way adjustable bridge, compromising intonation accuracy for the sake of simplicity. But since twelve-strings never play in tune anyway, who's going to notice? Rickenbacker strings its twelve-string guitars with the octave string "below," or to the right of the lower pitched string—opposite the usual practice.

Rickenbacker 660-12

Tools required: Intonation: 5/64" allen
Bridge height: 3/32" allen

The Rickenbacker 660 twelve-string with a twelve-way adjustable bridge—a necessity if one is serious about twelve-string intonation. 360 owners might consider converting to this bridge.

ARCHTOP ELECTRICS

Gibson ES-175

The bridge on this ES-175 features a compensated saddle. Notice the "setback" for the second string. This compensation works well with the heavier gauges (with a wound third string) used in jazz and rhythm styles, but very poorly with rock-and-roll strings.

D'Angelico

The bridges on electric archtop guitars like this D'Angelico (lefty) are usually simple, with a straight saddle, pictured here, or with compensation only for the second string. String height is adjusted by the thumbwheels and overall intonation is set by sliding the bridge forward and back.

VIBRATO TAILPIECES

Fender Jaguar

Tools required: Spring tension: phillips screwdriver

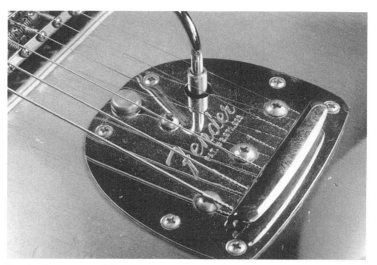

Fender Jaguars and Jazzmasters use a special vibrato tailpiece featuring a spring lock (the button between the two screws at the top) that can be pushed back to immobilize the vibrato. The spring tension is adjusted by the phillips screw directly to the left of the arm.

Fender Telecaster

Tools required: Bridge and saddle height: .050" allen
Intonation: phillips (flat-blade pictured)

Some Telecasters, such as the one pictured here, came stock with a Bigsby vibrato tailpiece. The bridge is similar to the ones used on the Jaguar and Jazzmaster. This model Bigsby with the extra roller in front was designed specifically for solidbody guitars. The vibrato arm position is controlled by shims beneath the spring.

Gretsch Country Gentleman

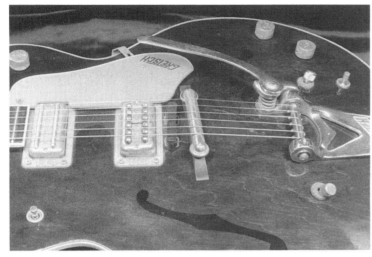

The Bigsby vibrato tailpiece shown on this Country Gentleman was widely used on various makes and models for many years. The arm height is adjusted by the use of shims beneath the spring. Note the mute, controlled by the two knobs on either side of the tailpiece.

LOCKING AND FINE-TUNING TREMOLO BRIDGES

Charvel Jackson 3

Tools required: Bridge height: 4mm allen
Intonation, string clamp: 3/32" allen

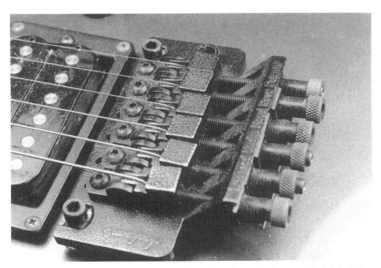

Floyd Rose-licensed Jackson tremolo bridge installed on a Model 3. The knurled knobs are for fine tuning, while the string-clamp allen screws run concentrically through the centers.

ESP Navigator

Tools required: Intonation: 1/16" allen
Bridge height: phillips screwdriver

A Floyd Rose-licensed Kahler bridge on an ESP Navigator. The intonation adjustments are beneath the strings. The fine-tuning thumbscrews point upwards, and the knurled knobs on the right lock the strings.

Fender Stratocaster

Tools required: Trem-arm tension, cam tension: 5/64" allen
String spacing, saddle height: .050" allen
Intonation: phillips screwdriver

The Kahler flat-mount tremolo bridge on a Stratocaster. The bridge fits into a recessed area in the body. This very popular bridge is fully adjustable.

Dean Bel Aire

Tools required: Trem-arm tension, cam tension: 5/64"
allen
String spacing, saddle height: .050" allen
Intonation: phillips screwdriver

The Kahler stud-mount version of their tremolo bridge, installed on a Dean Bel Aire. The overall height is adjusted by the thumbwheels in front and the studs in back. This bridge style replaces a stop-tailpiece/ Tune-O-Matic bridge combination (Kahler made the bridge for Gibson, too) and features adjustable string spacing and fine tuners.

Fender Heartfield Elan

Tools required: Bridge height: 3mm allen
Saddle intonation: 2mm allen
String lock: 9/64" allen

The Floyd Rose Pro model locking-tremolo bridge, installed on a Fender Heartfield Elan. All the standard features popularized by Rose, including string locks, fine tuning, fulcrum bridge pivots, and adjustable intonation are here. Saddle height adjustments, when necessary, are accomplished with thin metal shim stock.

Ibanez RG560

Tools required: String lock: 3mm allen
Bridge height: 4mm allen
Saddle position: 2mm allen

A Floyd Rose-licensed bridge on an Ibanez RG560. This bridge has all the usual Rose locking-trem/fine-tuner features.

Charvel Jackson Pro-1

Tools required: String lock, bridge height: 3mm allen
Saddle position: 2.5mm allen

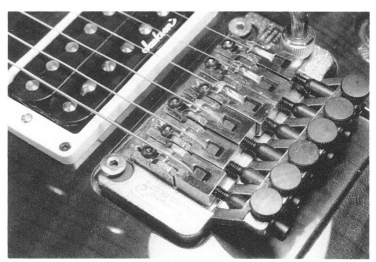

The Jackson Pro-1 has a Floyd Rose-licensed bridge made by Schaller. In addition to the usual locking-trem features, the bridge is inset into the body for additional tremolo range.

Washburn Signature

Tools required: Saddle position, bridge height: 5/64" allen
String lock: 3/32" allen

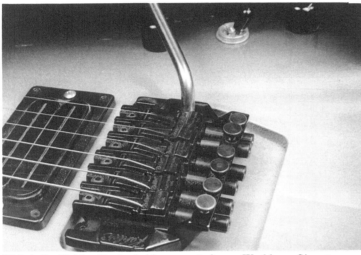

This is the Kahler Spyder bridge mounted on a Washburn Signature guitar. The fine-tuning bridge is inset into the body for extended tremolo range.

Kramer

Tools required: String lock: 3mm allen
Saddle lock: 2.5mm allen

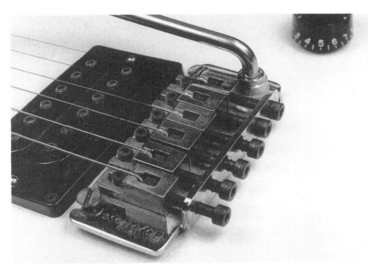

An early Floyd Rose locking-tremolo bridge on a Kramer guitar. All of the basic features of the locking-trem design are here except for the fine tuners. The fine tuners are now considered essential in order to avoid the hassle of having to unlock the nut to retune. But this was the first...

Fender Stratocaster Japanese Standard

Tools required: Bridge height: phillips screwdriver
Saddle height: .050" allen
Intonation: allen wrench beneath bridge (not shown)

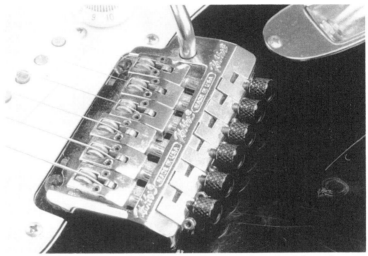

A Kahler fulcrum-tremolo bridge on a Japanese Standard Strat from the 80s. In addition to having intonation, bridge height, and saddle height adjustments, this bridge features string rollers and adjustable string spacing.

Fender Stratocaster

Tools required: Saddle height and rear cam: .050" allen
Saddle intonation, pitch change for each pair of strings, tremolo spring tension: 3/32" allen

The Washburn Wonder Bar on a Fender Stratocaster. This is a fine-tuning bridge with adjustments for everything, including pitch change for each pair of strings when using the tremolo. The tremolo arm can be switched over for left-hand use.

Peavey Mantis LT

Tools required: Saddle height and intonation: .050"
allen
Cam tension and arm tension: 5/64" allen

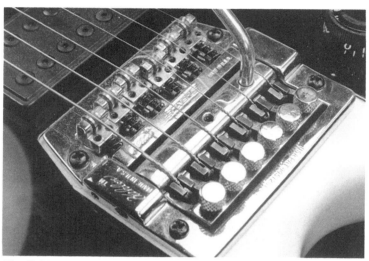

The Kahler Flyer is a less expensive version of the well-known Kahler flat-mount bridge. This one is mounted on a Peavey Mantis LT.

ELECTRIC BASSES

Fender Precision

Tools required: Saddle height: 1.5mm allen
Intonation: phillips screwdriver

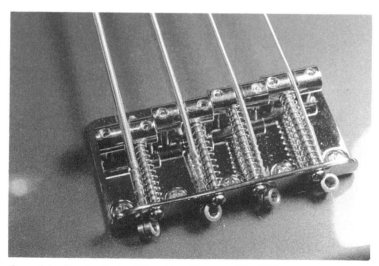

One of the Fender import Precision Bass models. This bridge is typical of the adjustable models used on the Precision and Jazz Basses. It is simple yet fully adjustable. A classic design.

Fender Jazz Bass with Badass bridge

Tools required: Saddle height: .050" allen
Intonation: flat-blade screwdriver

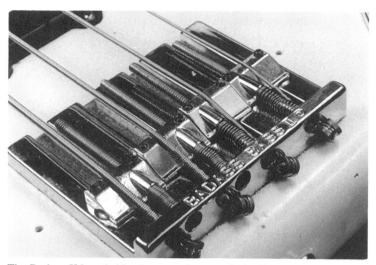

The Badass II bass bridge is a popular retrofit for Fender-style basses. Full adjustability and very long intonation adjustment range make it adaptable to any string and action combination.

Epiphone bass with Kahler tremolo bridge

Tools required: String spacing, saddle height: 1/16"
allen
Tremolo spring: 5/64" allen

The Kahler tremolo bass bridge installed on an Epiphone bass. Tremolo bridges are relatively rare on basses.

Steinberger

Tools required: Saddle height and lock: 2mm allen

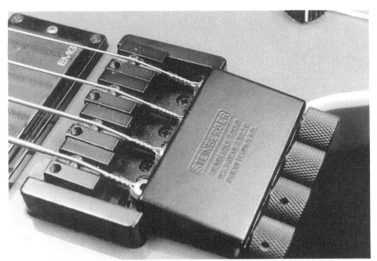

The Steinberger bass bridge. The knurled thumbscrews are for overall tuning.

Gibson Firebird

Tools required: Bridge height: large flat-blade screwdriver
Intonation: phillips screwdriver

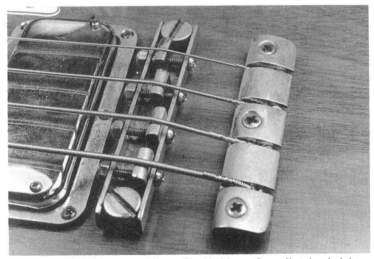

An adjustable bridge on a Gibson Firebird bass. Overall string height can be adjusted via the large screws on the ends. Intonation range is very limited.

Gibson Victory

Tools required: All adjustments: flat-blade screwdriver

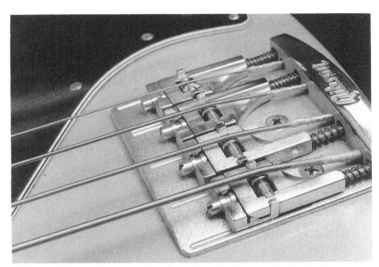

Gibson's Victory bass, produced during the 80s, used a bridge by Schaller. The string spacing is adjusted by means of the roller saddles, while string height is set by a screw working on a cam beneath each saddle.

Fender Precision

Tools required: Intonation: phillips screwdriver
Saddle height: 5/64" allen

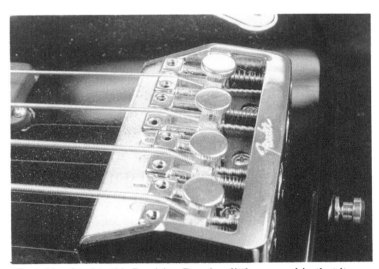

The bridge fitted to this Precision Bass is a little unusual in that it incorporates fine tuners. All of the usual intonation and saddle adjustments are provided.

Gibson Ripper

Tools required: All adjustments: flat-blade screwdriver

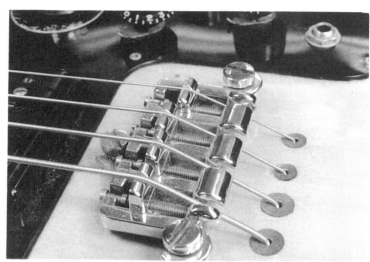

Gibson's fully adjustable three-point bridge was used on many of their basses. This one is fitted to a Ripper. The middle (front) height-adjustment stud is for leveling the bridge base.

Rickenbacker 4001

Tools required: Bridge height: allen wrench
Intonation: phillips

The Rickenbacker 4001 bridge. Overall string height is adjusted via the allen screws at each end of the saddle base. Individual intonation adjustment is by phillips screwdriver behind each saddle. Access is difficult and range is limited; you may have to relocate the bridge assembly in order to intonate certain string/action combinations.

BOLT-ON NECKS

Fender Beck-model Stratocaster

Tools required: Neck angle: 1/8" allen

The current four-bolt Fender neck with the Micro-Tilt system. You can adjust the neck angle with an allen wrench, eliminating the need for shims. The Micro-Tilt was used on the earlier three-bolt necks as well.

Late 70s Fender Stratocaster

Tools required: Neck angle adjustment: 3/32" allen

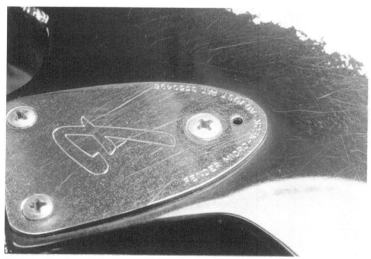

This is the three-bolt Micro-Tilt neck plate for a 70s Stratocaster. The adjusting screw is reached through the hole in the plate next to the phillips screw head. Though not as stable as a four-bolt neck, this system is very convenient to adjust.

LOCKING NUTS AND STRING LOCKS

Fender Stratocaster Japanese Standard

Tools required: 3/32" allen

The Kahler locking nut on an 80s Japanese Standard Strat. The strings feed through slots in the rear of the nut, maintaining downward pressure and eliminating the need for an additional string bar.

Fender Heartfield Elan

Tools required: String clamp: 3mm allen
Nut mounting screws: 2.5mm allen

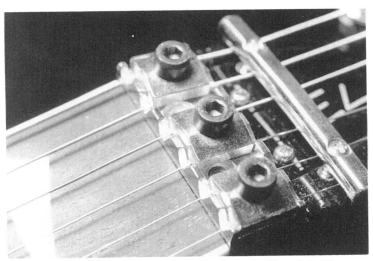

The popular Floyd Rose locking nut, installed on a Heartfield Elan. Each clamp locks two strings. The bar behind the nut maintains constant downward pressure on the strings, minimizing detuning when the strings are unlocked. On retrofit conversions, these nuts require careful fitting.

ESP Navigator

Tools required: String clamp: Straight-blade screw-driver

A Kahler "Flip Latchnut" string lock on an ESP Navigator. The screw over each pair of strings is adjusted so that it locks the pair when the latch is pushed down (as in the middle pair). When the latch is flipped up, the strings are released for tuning.

Fender Stratocaster

Tools required: String lock: 3/32" allen

The Kahler string lock on a Stratocaster. Each allen screw clamps a plate locking two strings. This type of string lock uses the original saddle, in contrast to the Floyd Rose style, which calls for replacement of the nut itself.

TRUSSRODS

Rickenbacker 660-12 Tom Petty Signature model

Tools required: 1/4" wrench

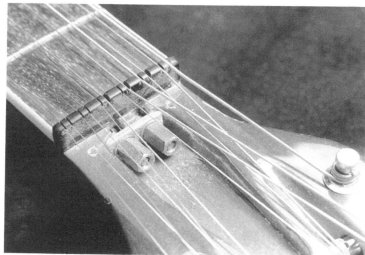

Rickenbacker twelve-strings have two trussrods. Adjust the tension evenly on both rods. Clearance is very limited at the nuts; you may have to modify an open-end or box wrench in order to get a fit. Rick twelve-strings are factory-fitted with the octave strings on the "bottom" (the opposite of conventional practice). In the photo the stringing is stock except for the fifth pair, which has (oops!) been reversed.

Mosrite 6-string

Tools required: 1/4" nutdriver

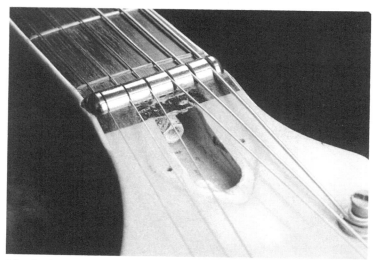

Mosrite is one of a handful of makers who use a zero fret. It determines string height, while the nut determines spacing.

Peavey T-60

Tools required: 5/16" nutdriver

Fender Stratocaster, late 70s

Tools required: 1/8" allen

Fender guitars were equipped with a bullet trussrod during the late 70s, replacing the adjustment position at the base of the neck.

Gretsch Country Gentleman

Tools required: Special wrench!

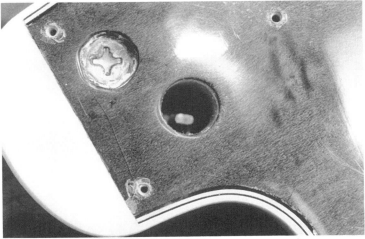

The Gretsch-Baldwin geared trussrod. This one is from a Country Gentleman. Finding a wrench to fit the shaft, which is 1-1/4" deep inside the hole, is going to be a problem. You can make one by getting a steel rod the same diameter as the hole size and cutting a slot in the end to fit the shaft. Bend the other end over to act as a handle.

Gibson L-5

Tools required: 5/16" nutdriver

Most Gibson trussrods are adjusted at the peghead; the 5/16" nutdriver size is standard.

Fender Stratocaster Mexican Standard

Tools required: 3/16" allen

Many import Fender Stratocasters, such as this Mexican Standard, take an allen wrench at the peghead for tension adjustment.

MISCELLANEOUS INTEREST

Paul Reed Smith locking machines

Paul Reed Smith's locking machine heads. The wings (levers) turn eccentrically around an inner cam, locking the string in place. Only half a turn is required, minimizing the tuning problems associated with multiple wraps loosening and tightening as the tremolo is used. The top thumbscrew is not an adjustment point.

Kubicki bass D-extension lever

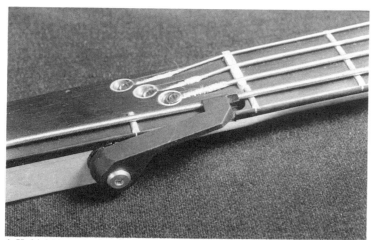

A Kubicki bass peghead, showing the D-to-E string lever. This feature is similar in concept to the C-extension found on double basses. If the string rattles when the lever is down check for a weak spring.

Kubicki bass bridge

Tools required: Intonation: phillips screwdriver
Saddle height: small wrench

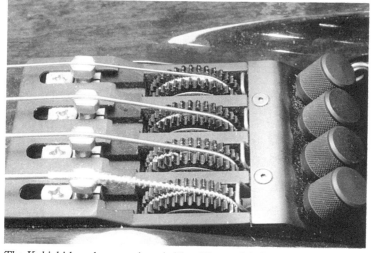

The Kubicki bass has a unique bridge. The neck is headless, with the strings tuned at the bridge instead. The saddles are individually adjustable for height (turn the slotted saddle head) and intonation (turn the phillips screw clockwise to loosen). To remove a string, detune, push the wire clip toward the tuner, and pull the string free. To restring, detune completely, push the end of the string into the hole in the middle of the gear and tighten the gear as tightly as possible by hand. Tuning to pitch can then be done with the tuning knob.

7
HIGH-TECH TREMOLO SYSTEMS

A SHORT HISTORY OF THE LOCKING TREMOLO

BY BILL STAPLETON

Popular music and the electric guitar grew up together and right along with them came the tremolo. A lot of great performers—the Ventures, Duane Eddy, Lonnie Mack, and Chet Atkins to name a very few—used the tremolo as a part of their signature sounds. And just as these great players were imitated, the sixties would bring a new star who would forever change the way tremolos and guitars would be played—right up to the present day.

Players who heard Jimi Hendrix for the first time were profoundly affected by his compositions and by his completely original approach to the instrument and use of feedback. A standout technique of his was the use of the tremolo arm, whether to add texture to his ballads, to embellish solos, or just let the guitar scream its feedbacking head off. Jimi Hendrix made the tremolo bar *walk and talk*...ladies and gentlemen.

I'm not here to say that it is impossible to use a standard tremolo unit and have it stay in tune. Hendrix would always try to retune after (or during!) a solo, and sometimes he got it right back, too. Eric Johnson does an excellent job with a standard trem system. Perhaps the most amazing performances were done by Eddie Van Halen in his band's first big shows. He used a standard Strat bridge, a brass nut with wide string slots—and a can of Three-in-One oil.

As a player, I spent years learning the riffs and guitar language of Jimi Hendrix. No matter what venue I found myself in, a Hendrix tune always got great crowd reaction if the band performed it well. But the thing that always held you back, though, was using the trem when doing one of those wild solos. Chances of coming back into the verse or chorus in tune were remote, so you rarely took the chance to get *way outside*, you know...where it's fun!

I was privileged to witness one small part of guitar history in 1979 one rainy afternoon in San Francisco. A long-haired blond fella with a mustache came into the store I was working in and claimed that he had a Stratocaster that wouldn't go out of tune no matter how much you worked the tremolo arm... and was I interested in seeing it? "Only me and the rest of the world," I said.

He came back in with a fifties maple-necked Strat with the first locking bridge and nut (ever) on it. Floyd Rose was testing the waters on his new bridge. To be brief, we went absolutely crazy over it; we begged and pleaded for him to make us some. Floyd agreed, and a short time later you could send a guitar to him in Seattle and he would install the bridge himself. Ahh— those were the days....

Great musicians all over the country lined up for those bridges (and the fine-tuning models that followed). The creativity of these players, combined with a trem that would stay in tune no matter what, led to some absolutely incredible music. Van Halen, most notably, changed the guitar's vocabulary for the next decade; his command of the "whammy bar," as the trem came to be known, and his unique tapping technique combined to rocket him to the top. Just like with Hendrix ten years earlier, everyone wanted to play like Van Halen.

What exactly is it that players are trying to achieve with all this high-tech machined hardware? To name a few techniques, the player can vibrato an entire chord (strummed or plucked), and lower or raise notes in a given phrase to create different textures. In rock playing, sustained or repeated trills can be dropped or raised; natural and false harmonics (clean or distorted) take on new voices. You can drop the low E or A string a full octave and return to pitch (entire phrases can be played on a single string, with the trem arm acting as a pitch control). One great trick is to depress the tremolo arm so that the strings are very loose—almost flapping on the neck—then hit the B or G string fifth fret harmonic while muting the other strings (your amp on full blast is best) and raise the bar very slowly to the original tuning, and then pull up or back another step or so.... You get a great siren effect, folks...yeah, that's entertainment!

The locking tremolo is great for all kinds of noises. Groans, growls, shrieks, whale sounds, sustaining feedback, and other mayhem can now be thrown into any given song or solo. You can do any or all of this stuff and the guitar is still in tune.

Yes, it is possible to do these things with the old-style tremolos, but the guitar would then be completely out of tune. The wound strings would pass through the nut when you depressed the tremolo arm, but on the return trip the windings would catch on the nut. Players who use a lot of string turns on the posts of the machines give the strings another opportunity to loosen and tighten unevenly. String retainers, Tune-O-Matic saddles, Bigsby dual-roller bridges, extra string length between the bridge saddle and tailpiece.... Practically anything that comes into contact with the string but doesn't hold it is a potential place for the string to hang up on.

What Floyd Rose did was to eliminate all the obstructions and clamp the strings at the very points where they go over the nut and the bridge saddle. Where the Floyd can do an octave change easily, the older-style tremolos like the Bigsby might give you a step and a half if you really stand on them.

I had an original Floyd without the fine tuners; it took a fair amount of monkeying around with a strobe tuner before a gig to get right in tune. Even then, you'd still have to tune some strings sharp and some flat before clamping because the locking nut affected each string differently when it compressed them. You would thing they would all go the same direction (either sharp or flat) but they didn't. If you wanted to retune during a set, it was not easy to do quickly since you had to unlock the nut in order to retune with the machines. Ultimately, the fine-tuner addition to the original design was the answer.

The Kramer Guitar Company was not setting the world on fire in the early eighties. Their brown-and-blond glued-together bodies and metal necks were not for everyone. Floyd Rose approached Fender first with his idea (they couldn't see it); when Rose and Van Halen entered the Kramer picture...Presto!...instant success. Kramer became an overnight giant, everybody wanted one, and practically all models came with a Rose bridge starting at $250!

At this point ("Everybody wants to get into the act!", as Jimmy Durante would say), another great machinist came along. Gary Kahler went at the tremolo equation from a different angle. A complaint against the Floyd Rose system is that if you rest your palm on the bridge itself, it will fluctuate in pitch. Many players can't break the habit. Kahler's spring-loaded cam, set behind the fixed bridge-pieces, allows you to rest your palm on the bridge and still use a locking system. The cam Kahlers do not have the wide range in pitch change that the Floyds do, and produce a somewhat muted sound, but Kahler's fulcrum-and-cam bridges are now used by a wide variety of guitar makers. Although until recently the original Floyd Rose bridges were found only on Kramer guitars, many companies now produce locking tremolo bridges under license to Rose. The original Rose bridges are currently available on Fender guitars and are in the Fender parts catalog.

The locking tremolo adds many new sentences to the vocabulary of guitar playing. No single invention can make or break a player; it is the mastery of many techniques and the ability to speak in many voices that makes the great player. The more help a guitarist has from his equipment, the more time he has to concentrate on creating. The locking tremolo is an invention I waited a long time for. Thanks, Floyd.

Locking Tremolo Tips

While locking trems are great for staying in tune compared to the traditional units, you still have to observe a certain amount of trem protocol. Clamp the strings firmly, but don't overtighten. The integrity of a string's metal core can be damaged by overtightening, causing string breakage and tuning difficulty. Overtightening also is darn hard on the hex nuts (string clamps). Just because something is tightened to death doesn't mean it won't go out of tune.

Reset the fine tuners before you clamp the strings. When using double locking bridges, remove the ball end by cutting it above any winding or reinforced winding that may secure it. Try to cut clean with sharp cutters; dull cutters or pulling while cutting the string will loosen the winding from the string core. This can give a loose fit on the clamp and make the string sound dead.

And probably the most important point of all is to stretch the heck out of those strings both before and after clamping the nut lock. After all, this is a guitar string we're dealing with here, and they *do* stretch no matter what. Finally, leave your instrument on stage for as long as possible before you fine-tune and perform. Stage temperature and humidity often differs greatly from backstage, dressing room, and equipment truck.

A Closer Look at the Locking Tremolo Bridge: The Floyd Rose and Kahler Bridges

Locking tremolo bridges are quite complicated, as far as guitar bridges go, and require some basic setup work in order to get the most out of them. In the following paragraphs are setup instructions for two of the most popular systems in use today. Both the fulcrum-style Floyd Rose bridge and the Kahler fulcrum-and-cam-style bridges are widely used on both older and current instruments. In addition, many companies produce bridges under Floyd Rose license (including Kahler), so the instructions given here can generally be applied to other makes as well.

Floyd Rose bridges

The Floyd Rose bridges operate, in general terms, in the same way as the standard Stratocaster tremolo bridges. For a review of the adjustment procedure for the Stratocaster bridge, see Chapter 2. Building upon the design of the Strat bridge, the Rose bridge uses a "knife-edge" fulcrum pivot on the bridge base and two pivot screws (or studs on some variations). The saddles are supplied in three different heights, providing an arc to match the fingerboard radius. Instead of being threaded through the bottom of the tremolo block, the strings are clamped directly into the saddles. Except for the very first models, all bridges have provisions for fine-tuning each string.

The fulcrum pivot arrangement with just two screws provides smooth operation with less friction than the traditional bridge. The pivot screws are also used for basic height adjustments and are adjusted first when setting the basic action.

For most situations the basic height adjustments with the pivot screws are all that is necessary. If after you check the action for each string, you find that further individual string-height adjustments are necessary, remove the saddles and shim them up with shim stock so that they follow the radius of the fingerboard. You can get shim stock in an automotive or machine shop, or (for convenience) you can cut up a set of feeler gauges, since you probably will be shimming only one or two saddles anyway. While shimming saddles is not as convenient as setting the height with adjustment screws, the Rose saddles, because they are securely bolted down, will give better sustain and stay permanently in adjustment.

As with a traditional bridge, set the bridge plate level or parallel with the top by adjusting the number and tension of the tremolo springs, even if the bridge has been recessed into the top. If your guitar doesn't have a recess, you may want to consider this modification if you want more upward pitch change.

Adjust intonation by loosening the set screw holding the saddle down and sliding the saddle forward and back as required. Since there is no intonation adjustment screw to hold the saddle in place when the saddle set screw is loosened, you will have to use a little ingenuity when setting intonation. Though you could loosen the string when moving the saddle to its new position, the more convenient way is to use the tremolo to take all the tension off the strings ("dump" or "dive-bomb") by pushing the tremolo arm all the way down. While the strings are loose, move the saddle to the new position and lock it down. As soon as you loosen tension on the arm, you can recheck your intonation without having to retighten the string. Note that there are two positions for the saddle mounting screw. Some of the saddles, such as the ones for the third and sixth strings, may need to be held down with the screw in the rear position.

Kahler bridges

These are made in two styles. The fulcrum pivot models, which are licensed by Floyd Rose, are adjusted, for the most part, in the same way as the Rose tremolo. There are actually quite a few variations. Some, for example, have an adjustment screw for intonation in addition to a saddle mounting screw.

The cam-style flat mount, while different from the Floyd Rose style, is straightforward to set up. String spacing, intonation, and individual string height are all ajustable with set screws. The saddles can be slid back and forth for intonation without the bother of trying to keep the string tension from pushing the saddle forward. Spring tension is set from the top.

Appendix A
Neck Relief

A guitar neck with proper relief accomodates the motion of a vibrating string. It should not be absolutely straight; instead, it should have a slight parabolic curve. Examples of parabolic curves include the center span of a suspension bridge, a rope hanging between two posts, and a guitar string held loosely in your fingers. On a guitar the nut forms one of the points of suspension and the bridge saddle forms the other. The exact center of the span is at the twelfth fret. The relief required is the distance between the string and a straight line drawn between the center (twelfth fret) and one of the suspension points. This distance (relief) will vary depending upon the distance from the ends. More importantly, the relief will not change at an even rate, but at a rate determined by a parabolic equation.

Ideally, the relief adjustment is good only for the open-string length. As soon as you start fretting higher up the fingerboard, the relief measurements get further away from the ideal. In practice this is not a problem, because the strings vibrate in a smaller arc as you fret up the fingerboard, offsetting errors in the relief settings. While other factors, such as higher overtones, stiffness of the strings (the "end effect"), and even picking style, also affect the relief settings, the main influence is the fundamental (parabolic) vibration of the string.

Neck Relief

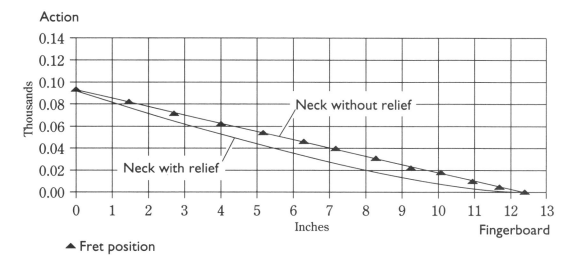

Relief Calculations: 0-12th Frets

Action 64ths	1000ths height in inches	(nut) 0	1	2	3	4	5	Fret Intervals 6	7	8	9	10	11	12
1.0	0.016	0.000	0.001	0.002	0.003	0.003	0.003	0.003	0.003	0.003	0.002	0.002	0.001	0.000
2.0	0.031	0.000	0.002	0.004	0.005	0.006	0.007	0.007	0.006	0.006	0.005	0.004	0.002	0.000
3.0	0.047	0.000	0.003	0.006	0.008	0.009	0.010	0.010	0.010	0.009	0.007	0.005	0.003	0.000
4.0	0.063	0.000	0.004	0.008	0.010	0.012	0.013	0.013	0.013	0.012	0.010	0.007	0.004	0.000
5.0	0.078	0.000	0.006	0.010	0.013	0.015	0.016	0.017	0.016	0.015	0.012	0.009	0.005	0.000
6.0	0.094	0.000	0.007	0.012	0.015	0.018	0.020	0.020	0.019	0.017	0.015	0.011	0.006	0.000
7.0	0.109	0.000	0.008	0.014	0.018	0.021	0.023	0.023	0.022	0.020	0.017	0.013	0.007	0.000
8.0	0.125	0.000	0.009	0.016	0.021	0.024	0.026	0.026	0.026	0.023	0.019	0.014	0.008	0.000
9.0	0.141	0.000	0.010	0.017	0.023	0.027	0.029	0.030	0.029	0.026	0.022	0.016	0.009	0.000
10.0	0.156	0.000	0.011	0.019	0.026	0.030	0.033	0.033	0.032	0.029	0.024	0.018	0.010	0.000
11.0	0.172	0.000	0.012	0.021	0.028	0.033	0.036	0.036	0.035	0.032	0.027	0.020	0.011	0.000
12.0	0.188	0.000	0.013	0.023	0.031	0.036	0.039	0.040	0.038	0.035	0.029	0.022	0.012	0.000

APPENDIX B
THE FRET TESTER

Finding out which fret or group of frets is causing buzzes is just about impossible without some sort of electronic aid. One of the best ways to locate fret buzzes is to use a multimeter, set on a resistance range, to check continuity between a string and a suspected fret. This method will only work with metal strings or strings with a metal wrapping.

You will need a multimeter (either analog or digital) that can measure resistance. If your meter has several range settings, set it on the highest resistance range. [6398-9] Use test leads with a clip built into the end so that you will be able to clip one lead to a string. And finally, get a capo so that you can stop the string wherever you want to test a fret.

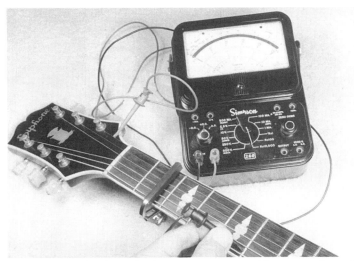

Fret tester: To check out fret buzzes, you can use either an analog-style multimeter (shown) or a digital model. This testing method is simple and it really works.

Clip one lead to the string you want to test. This can go between the nut and the machine head, or between the

saddle and the tailpiece. Put the capo on the fret position that you want to test. In other words, if you are getting a fret buzz when the string is fretted at the second fret, put the capo behind the second fret.

Now play the string, holding the guitar in normal playing position so that the buzz is reproduced. While you are playing, hold the second test lead with your free hand against each fret that you want to test. Wherever the string is buzzing against a fret, it will complete the resistance circuit and you will get a reading. The actual resistance reading is not important, though the relative measurement will give you an idea of the severity of the buzz. If the string is buzzing badly on the fret being tested, the resistance measurement will be lower than on a fret where it is just barely making contact.

If fret buzzes occur when you play at other frets, move the capo to the other positions and again check for readings. Make a note of every fret that is causing a buzz (check the other strings too) so you will know which frets need leveling. Don't be surprised to find a string buzzing on several frets at one time!

When you need to test the nylon strings on a classical guitar, temporarily substitute a steel string for the nylon string you want to check. If you do this one at a time (don't change all of the strings at one time), the overall tension on the neck and top will remain fairly constant and you won't do any harm to the guitar. Keep in mind that, given the nature of nylon strings, the action used on classical guitars and the construction of the guitar itself, fret buzzes on the first, second, and third strings of a classical guitar require this type of testing very rarely indeed.

INDEX